MW01679462

CAMBRIDGE

CHECKPOINTS 2015

VCE English/EAL
Using Language to Persuade

- Language analysis
- Oral presentations
- Writing point-of-view texts

Andrea Hayes

CAMBRIDGE
UNIVERSITY PRESS

CAMBRIDGE
UNIVERSITY PRESS

477 Williamstown Road, Port Melbourne, VIC 3207, Australia

Cambridge University Press is part of the University of Cambridge.

It furthers the University's mission by disseminating knowledge in the pursuit of education, learning and research at the highest international levels of excellence.

www.cambridge.edu.au
Information on this title: www.cambridge.org/9781107484528

First published 2015

Printed in Australia by Ligare Pty Ltd

A Cataloguing-in-Publication entry is available from the catalogue of the National Library of Australia at www.nla.gov.au

ISBN 978-1-107-48452-8 Paperback

Additional resources for this publication at www.cambridge.edu.au/vcecheckpoints

Contents

Introduction

You don't have to be super brilliant or creative to produce high-scoring language analyses, oral presentations or written point-of-view texts. Analysing media texts, creating point-of-view (persuasive texts) texts and delivering effective oral presentations are skills you can practise and learn. A student who plans, reads carefully, listens to their English teacher's advice and follows the steps and hints in this edition of Checkpoints will be able to avoid major stress and do well. Good luck!

Andrea Hayes

Acknowledgements

Andrea Hayes would like to thank the usual suspects: Luisa and John Catalano, Spike, Zeebo and Jennifer Blackburn, as well as Frankie Flanagan for her significant language analysis contributions, Jo Ellis for her EAL advice and sample analysis responses and Martin 'Hassa' Hayes for his illustrations, Mick Connolly for his comment, and Hayley Bunting for her sample language analysis response. She would also like to thank Luisa Catalano, Sarah Jackson, George Longbottom, Chen Qian for their sample oral presentations and the staff and students at Brighton Grammar School, especially her Year 11 and 12 classes, for their support.

VCE survival tips

1. Be committed – attend practice exams and participate in classes.
2. Take responsibility for your own learning, e.g. submit extra drafts.
3. Start a media diet, e.g. 10–15 minutes daily reading online or print newspapers and watching TV news so that you are up to date with topical issues, words used in media texts and different writing styles.
4. Organise a workable study schedule with some 'chill time'.
5. Identify weak areas and set goals to improve, e.g. 'to better describe the likely impact on the audience'.
6. Ensure that you know SAC and exam conditions and assessment criteria.
7. Discuss topical issues with classmates and teachers, and identify different points of view and arguments.
8. Bond with your dictionary (the latest edition from a well-respected publisher) and develop lists of analysis verbs and words used in the media.
9. Research examples of effective speeches and analyse the conventions used, e.g. those by Barack Obama, Quentin Bryce and Paul Keating.
10. Realise that stress is normal, but avoid drugs and try not to fall in love (it is too distracting)!

Chapter 1

Course overview

The three Areas of Study in Units 3 and 4 are:

- Reading and responding (Text response)
- Creating and presenting (Context writing)
- Using language to persuade (Language analysis).

Each Area of Study has outcomes that you achieve by completing assessment tasks. In order to successfully complete assessment tasks you need to learn sets of knowledge and skills. The knowledge and skills have a lot of overlap. For example, in 'Using language to persuade' you learn to identify persuasive language and techniques. You will need to use some of these techniques when you create your own oral presentation or written point-of-view text. Of course, language skills, including correct spelling, punctuation and grammar, are always required in each Area of Study.

Units 3 and 4 are assessed by SACs (School Assessed Coursework) and each unit is marked out of 100 marks and worth 25% of your study score. The end of year exam is worth 50%. EAL stands for English as Additional Language.

Unit 3 (25%) overview

Outcome 100 marks	**Assessment task**	**EAL Assessment task**
1	Analytical text response (written or oral). 30 marks	Analytical text response (written or oral). 35 marks
2	One sustained or three to five shorter texts created for one or more specific audiences and context *plus* written explanation of decisions about form, purpose, language, audience and context. 30 marks	One sustained or three to five shorter texts created for a specific audience(s) and context. 30 marks
3	Language analysis of three or more persuasive texts *and* (written or oral) point-of-view text on selected issue. 20 marks each = 40 marks	Point-of-view text on selected issue (written or oral). 35 marks

Unit 4 (25%) overview

Outcome 100 marks	Assessment task	EAL Assessment task
1	Extended written interpretation of one selected text. 50 marks	Extended written interpretation of one selected text. 50 marks
2	One sustained or three to five shorter texts created for a specific audience(s) and context *plus* written explanation of decisions made about form, purpose, language, audience and context. 50 marks	One sustained or three to five shorter texts created for a specific audience(s) and context. 50 marks

There is no language analysis SAC in Unit 4.

End-of-year examination (50%)

	Assessment tasks	EAL assessment tasks
Section A	One extended analytical/ expository text response to texts from List 1.	One extended analytical/ Expository text response to texts from List 1.
Section B	One extended piece (expository, persuasive, imaginative) using ideas from selected Context and direct reference to at least one text from Context.	One extended piece (expository, persuasive, imaginative) using ideas from selected Context and direct reference to at least one text from Context.
Section C	One extended analysis of written language and visual features in unseen text(s).	Part 1 Note-form summary. Part 2 Analysis of how written language and visual features persuade readers about three main points in summary.

[VCAA Study Design 2007–2015]

Assessment Unit 3 SAC Mainstream

Outcome 3

Analyse the use of language in texts that present a point of view on an issue currently debated in the Australian media, and to construct, orally or in writing, a sustained and reasoned point of view on the selected issue.

Task 1

Mark range	Descriptor: typical performance in each range
17–20 marks	Sophisticated analysis and insightful comparison of the ways in which the language of selected persuasive texts is used to position readers in particular ways. Highly expressive and coherent writing with confident use of highly appropriate metalanguage.
13–16 marks	Detailed analysis and careful comparison of the ways in which the language of selected persuasive texts is used to position readers in particular ways. Expressive, coherent and fluent writing and relevant use of appropriate metalanguage.
9–12 marks	Analysis and some comparison of the ways in which the language of selected persuasive texts is used to position readers in particular ways. Generally expressive, fluent and coherent writing and mostly relevant use of appropriate metalanguage.
5–8 marks	Some analysis and limited comparison of the ways in which the language of selected persuasive texts is used to position readers in particular ways. Clear written expression and some use of appropriate metalanguage.
1–4 marks	Little analysis or comparison of the ways in which the language of selected persuasive texts is used to position readers in particular ways. Simple written expression and limited use of appropriate metalanguage.

Task 2 Oral or written

Mark range	Descriptor: typical performance in each range
17–20 marks	Presentation of complex ideas in a sustained, coherent and logical argument. In an oral response, the skilful use of highly appropriate oral language conventions to engage an audience. Highly expressive, coherent and fluent written response. Accurate and detailed acknowledgment of sources where appropriate.
13–16 marks	A sustained, coherent and logical argument. In an oral response, an ability to use appropriate oral language conventions to engage an audience. Expressive, coherent and fluent written response. Acknowledgment of sources where appropriate.
9–12 marks	An argument which is generally sustained and coherent. In an oral response, an ability to use some appropriate oral language conventions to engage an audience. Generally expressive, coherent and fluent written response. Acknowledgment of some sources where appropriate.
5–8 marks	A superficial argument. In an oral response, variable ability to use oral language conventions to engage an audience. Clear expression of ideas in writing. Limited acknowledgment of sources.
1–4 marks	Little sense of argument. In an oral response, limited use of oral language conventions to engage an audience. Simple expression of ideas in writing. Little or no acknowledgment of sources.

[VCE English/EAL Assessment Handbook 2008–2015, pp. 20–21]

Written examination – end of year

Section C – Language analysis (Using language to persuade)
Holistic descriptors

- Understanding of the ideas and points of view presented
- Analysis of ways in which language and visual features are used to present a point of view and to persuade readers
- Controlled and effective use of language appropriate to the task

Assessors mark holistically, relating student performance to the published criteria and ranking student responses over the full range of marks available. Determination of the mark is assisted by descriptors of Expected Qualities for the Mark Range; these have been written to reflect the level of achievement expected at a particular mark or mark range.

Expected qualities for the mark range – Section C

The mark range corresponds to the student response in the following way.

9–10 Shows a perceptive and sophisticated understanding of a range of ways in which the written and visual language positions readers in the context presented. Develops a cogent, controlled and well-substantiated analysis using precise and effective language and expression.

8 Shows a highly developed understanding of a range of ways in which the written and visual language positions readers in the context presented. Develops a detailed, substantiated and coherent analysis using language and expression fluently and confidently.

7 Shows an understanding of how the written and visual language seeks to position readers, with reference to the context presented. Achieves a planned and supported response using accurate language and clear expression.

6 Shows some understanding of how written and visual language is used and some awareness of the context presented. Achieves a planned and supported response, generally using accurate language and expression.

5 Shows some understanding of how language is used and an awareness of the context of the written and visual material presented. Attempts a planned and supported piece of writing using adequate language and expression.

4 Shows limited understanding of how language is used and little awareness of the context presented. Presents a piece of writing with little organisation and basic language and expression.

3 Shows limited knowledge of how language is used in the construction of written and visual texts. Demonstrates basic expression and language control.

1–2 Shows very limited knowledge of how language is used. Demonstrates some expression and language control.

0 Shows no understanding of the requirements of the task.

[2009 English criteria and descriptors, Version 2]

Assessment Unit 3 – EAL SAC

Outcome 3 Oral or written

Analyse the use of language in texts that present a point of view on an issue currently debated in the Australian media, and to construct, orally or in writing, a sustained and reasoned point of view on the selected issue.

Mark range	Descriptor: typical performance in each range
29–35 marks	Thorough and detailed knowledge of the issue and highly appropriate selection of evidence to support argument. Presentation of a highly developed, coherent and logical argument. In an oral response, skilful use of appropriate oral language conventions to engage an audience. For a written response, highly organised, fluent and sustained writing with excellent control of the conventions of written English. Detailed acknowledgment of sources where appropriate.
22–28 marks	Sound knowledge of the issue and appropriate selection of evidence to support argument. Soundly developed and generally coherent and logical argument. In an oral response, good use of appropriate oral language conventions to engage an audience. For a written response, organised, fluent and relevant writing with good control of the conventions of written English. Acknowledgment of sources where appropriate.
15–21 marks	Knowledge of the issue and generally appropriate selection of evidence to support argument. Presentation of an argument which is generally sustained and coherent. In an oral response,

	use of appropriate oral language conventions to engage an audience. For a written response, organised and relevant writing with sound control of the conventions of written English. Some acknowledgment of sources.
8–14 marks	Some knowledge of the issue and selection of some evidence to support argument. A superficial argument. In an oral response, attempted use of oral language conventions to engage an audience. For a written response, some use of oral language conventions to engage an audience. Limited acknowledgment of sources.
1–7 marks	Limited knowledge of the issue and little evidence used to support argument. Little sense of argument. In an oral response, limited use of oral language conventions. For a written response, limited organisation and control of the conventions of written English. Little or no acknowledgment of sources.

[VCE English/EAL Assessment Handbook 2008–2015, pp 31–32]

EAL Written examination – end of year

Section C – Analysis of language use (Using language to persuade)

- Understanding of the ideas and points of view in the material presented
- Analysis of ways in which language and visual features are used to present a point of view and to persuade readers
- Control of the mechanics of the English language to support meaning

Except for the note-taking task, assessment is holistic, using the published criteria.

Expected qualities for the mark range – Section C

Part 1 – Clarity and accuracy in note taking

The following allocation of marks will be used as a guide:

- 5 marks for the main points
- 2 marks for the use of note-form
- 3 marks for the clarity and conciseness of the response.

Part 2 – Analysis of the language use
The mark range corresponds to the student response in the following way.

9–10 Shows a sophisticated understanding of a range of ways in which the written and visual language positions readers in the context presented. Develops a detailed and well-substantiated analysis using fluent, precise and effective language and expression.

8 Shows a strong understanding of a range of ways in which the written and visual language positions readers in the context presented. Develops a substantiated and coherent analysis using fluent and effective language and expression.

7 Shows understanding of some ways in which the written and visual material seeks to position readers in the context presented. Achieves an organised and supported response with sound control of language and effective expression.

6 Shows some understanding of how written and visual language is used to persuade readers with some awareness of the context presented. Achieves a generally organised and supported response with general control of language and expression.

5 Shows some understanding of how language is used to persuade, and some awareness of the context of the written and visual material presented. Attempts a supported piece of writing using adequate language and expression.

4 Shows limited understanding of how language is used to persuade and limited awareness of the context presented. Attempts a piece of writing that offers some support for its points, and has some control of language and expression.

3 Shows limited knowledge of how language is used in written and visual texts. Demonstrates limited control of language and expression.

1–2 Shows a very limited knowledge of how language is used. Demonstrates very limited control of language and expression.

0 Shows no understanding of the requirements of the task.

[2009 ESL criteria and descriptors]

FAQs

1 Do I write about visual language in a separate paragraph?
No. Weave analysis of visual text(s) into your analysis where it supports arguments or main points.

2 Where's the best place to find the contention?
Obvious places to look include the headline, in the byline of an article, and at the start of a speech. Sometimes half of the contention may be at the beginning and the rest in the second-to-last paragraph of a text.

3 How do I identify tone?
Ask yourself, 'How does the author sound about the issue?' Do they sound angry? Smug? Positive? See Chapter 4 for a Tone chart that includes questions to ask to describe tone. See Chapter 2 for samples of tone and tonal shift language to use in your analysis. Analysing tone and tonal shifts is very important.

4 What is a tonal shift?
A tonal shift is when the author's tone changes. In a speech, for example, the author may begin using an upbeat or positive tone to connect with their audience, then they may refer to some statistics intended to shock the audience and change their tone to an ominous (warning) one. See Chapter 2 for samples of tone and tonal shift language to use in your analysis. Analysing tone and tonal shifts is very important.

5 Do I have to include every single persuasive technique?
No. That's impossible. Be selective and include only the language and techniques that best relate to contention, main points of the overall argument, appeals and tone.

6 What do I call the writer: 'the writer' or 'the author'?
Neither, if you know writer's name. Use first name and surname, e.g. Sam McQueen, the first time you use it, then refer to writer by surname, e.g. McQueen. Editorials have no writer's names. Refer to the author of a visual text as the 'creator'. The 2013 Exam was a newsletter and you could have written 'he', 'she', 'they' or 'the group' as author, as the name was not provided.

7 If there are two written texts, do I analyse them separately?
Try to weave all texts together, at least in your introduction (**mini weave**).
Semi weave means use woven texts in the introduction and conclusion, but analyse them separately in body paragraphs. **Total weave** is when all texts are woven throughout your analysis. Avoid **block style**, i.e. analysing them separately.

8 What's the difference between 'compare' and 'contrast'?
'Compare' means looking for similarities. 'Contrast' means looking for differences.

9 How many quotes do I need? Can I write quotes in the intro?
Think 'quote fest'. However, avoid long quotes. Try to weave quotes into sentences. It's a good idea to find a small quote that states part of your contention and include it in your introduction.

10 How do I write about the likely impact on and the positioning of the audience?
First you need to stereotype your audience (see Chapter 2) and put yourself in their shoes. Second, ask yourself how they are likely to think, believe, feel, act about an issue (the impact). Use different audience impact verbs e.g. provokes, encourages, appealing, shock.

11 What do I write in my conclusion?
Restate the contention(s). Comment on overall language style(s) and their likely impact on the audience of the texts. The conclusion is shorter than your introduction. You should not introduce any new points. Do not judge or evaluate which text has the better arguments. Do not include your point of view.

12 What does 'holistic' mean?
'Holistic' means understanding the 'big picture' about an issue – its context, the author's approach, different points of view and the likely impact on target audience.

13 Do I have to include visuals in my oral presentation?
No. If you want to include visuals, ask yourself, 'Does the visual enhance my speech?' If the answer is 'No', leave it out. If you do include a PowerPoint or videoclip, make sure that you have checked it with teacher (in case it's offensive) and that clip is not too long.

14 Can I pretend to be someone else when I give my speech?
Yes, you can pretend to be a different persona *but* make sure that you are convincing in this role.

15 What if my handwriting is illegible?
If you know that your handwriting is difficult to read you need to adopt strategies that make it easier to read: experiment with different pens, try printing, concentrate on finishing the letters off properly, leave more space between words and cross out words with a neat single stroke.

If there is a recognisable problem and you require special consideration or to use a computer you need to speak to your VCE Coordinator and organise it asap.

Key terms (metalanguage) – language to persuade

Argument: points structured to persuade audience to author's point of view. Author may use several arguments in their text. Some refer to these arguments as main points.

Author: used in broadest sense to mean creators of print, non-print and multimodal texts, e.g. you can author a website. Not used in place of 'director'. [VCAA Study Design 2007–2015]

Audience: whoever reads, views or listens to a text. All texts are written for an intended or target audience. Sometimes the audience will be a varied one (e.g. students, parents and teachers).

Background information: (also called the context) the information supplied with texts for analysis (e.g. who wrote a blog, in response to what event or situation, and their intended audience. It may include the author's status or expertise). This may provide you with extremely important information about form, the audience and the purpose to include in your language analysis.

Bias: prejudice against a person, object or movement. It may be inherent or learned.

Blog: (weblog) an online journal that may contain print, visual and auditory matter.

Blogger: a person who writes a blog.

Broadsheet: a large-sized newspaper that deals with world, national and 'serious' news in depth and detail (e.g. *The Australian*). This definition is changing as newspapers change size and increasingly change to online products.

Byline: a line or several lines in a newspaper that includes author's name.

Caption: a heading under a visual text.

Contention: the central message that an author wants their audience to accept. See Chapter 2.

Conventions: the expected and acceptable guidelines about writing styles and forms, such as expected style features and formats for letters and media texts. Oral conventions include greeting the audience when delivering a speech.

Digital landscape: the environment where digital technology is being used.

Director: the person responsible for the overall look, mood and story-shape of a film or film clip.

Editing: the process of checking a text's overall structure, language, tone, style, presentation and consistency, as well as correcting spelling and punctuation errors (proofreading). See Chapter 6.

Embedded text: text within a text (e.g. an alternative viewpoint to a newspaper article included in a personal blog).

Event: something that happens or takes place. It is usually something important. Events give rise to issues (e.g. the occurrence of a bushfire, the AFL grand final or a shark attack.)

Ezine: an electronic magazine, delivered either via a website or in an email newsletter. [VCAA Study Design 2007–2015]

Figurative language: figures of speech that show representations or create images for the reader (e.g. similes, metaphors, personification and irony).

Followers: people who regularly read a blog.

Form: how texts look on paper or on screen, including their layout, structure and patterns of language. Different forms have different conventions, e.g. letter may have a letterhead and a logo at the top. Cartoons may have speech bubbles.

Forum: An opportunity to voice an opinion on an issue via the internet (such as chat forums) or print. It is sometimes used as another name for 'letters to the editor'.

Interpretation: reading and understanding a text at a deeper level in order to understand an author's/director's ideas, point of view and why a text has been constructed in a certain way.

Irony: a device by which a creator expresses a meaning contradictory to the stated one, e.g. as a character in a play speaking lines that are understood by the audience but not other characters.

Issue: a topic that can be discussed or debated because it has at least two sides to consider and several different points of view people can argue.

Media texts: persuasive texts that can be print, non-print or multimodal (e.g. a blog, editorial, newsletter or a transcript from an oral presentation). They are full of issues for the public to discuss or debate.

Metalanguage: language used to discuss the structural and stylistic features of texts (e.g. editorial, alliteration and headline). Also, language used to discuss actual language itself (e.g. grammatical terms like 'adjective').

Motif: an image that recurs through a text, occurring in patterns.

Multimodal texts: texts that combine different modes of language, such as print, visuals, sound and spoken word, as in film texts or computer presentation media. [VCAA Study Design 2007–2015]

Non-print texts: texts that have no print or visual images such as a speech or radio program. [VCAA Study Design 2007–2015]

Non-verbal: the way in which meaning is constructed and conveyed by body gesture and facial expression. Also refers to the visual language of layout and design, the choice of font and colour, and the use of framing, camera angles and shots and sound effects. [VCAA Study Design 2007–2015]

Objective: not influenced by personal opinion – the opposite to subjective.

Perspective: point of view or opinion on an issue, idea, argument or text.

Plagiarism: when you don't reference texts you have borrowed and claimed them as your own. This is unfair and unacceptable.

Platform: operating system or computer architecture or combination of both (e.g. mobile phone).

Point-of-view text: a text that contains an author's point of view, e.g. an editorial, article, letter, email, personal column or transcript of a speech.

Print texts: texts that are print only or print and visual images, such as novels, plays, scripts for TV, radio or film, transcripts of radio talkback. [VCAA Study Design 2007–2015]

Prose: writing or speech without a formal rhythm or pattern such as a novel.

Pseudonym: also called 'pen-name' or 'nom de plume'**.** A name assumed by a writer to protect their anonymity (e.g. Joanne Rowling wrote under the pen-name J. K. Rowling for her Harry Potter series and more recently used the pseudonym 'Robert Galbraith' for her crime fiction novel for adults, *The Cuckoo's Calling*.

Purpose: the reason why a text is created (e.g. to analyse, inform, protest or recommend).

Register: describes the language used in particular situations and changes depending on the situation or context, topic and people involved. Your register may be public or private, spoken or written, formal or informal. Your register for your oral presentation may be public, spoken and formal.

Shock jock: a radio announcer who aims at a general audience and gains listeners' attention by being emotional, controversial and strongly opinionated.

Social media: media for social interaction using various online technology tools that enable people to communicate easily (e.g. Facebook, Twitter, YouTube, LinkedIn and blogs).

Sound grab: brief sound clip (e.g. a 20-word quote from a medical expert on the radio).

Style: the look, mood and feel of a text. It includes tone, voice, point of view, language, genre and conventions, plus specific techniques, features or stylistic devices related to the text type, e.g. personal voice in an opinion column, the type of brushstrokes or a motif in a cartoon.

Subjective: influenced by personal opinion – opposite to objective.

Subtext: the text or meaning that lies under the surface of a text; sometimes found by 'reading between the lines'.

Symbolism: the use of images or words to represent a deeper contextual meaning (e.g. water meaning life, a dove meaning peace, a 'skull and crossbones' meaning poison).

Tabloid: a text – print or online – that aims at a general audience. Often has many photos, a larger typeface and smaller page size than a broadsheet (e.g. *Herald Sun*).

Text type: a group of texts grouped according to different forms and genres, such as media with its different forms (e.g. an editorial, letter, feature article, opinion column or blog).

Tonal shift: when the tone changes in a tone, e.g. from a friendly tone to a concerned tone.

Tone: the attitude of the author or director towards a subject. Tone is implicit in language use and may be described variously as aggressive, sympathetic, passionate and so on.

Tweet: brief, 140-character text on the social networking platform *Twitter.*

Values: moral purpose and beliefs upheld by people e.g. 'always be honest', 'work hard and you will be rewarded', 'do your best', 'respect other people's opinions even if they are not the same as yours'. Three types are to be considered when studying VCE texts: (1) cultural values: values originating from the same culture; (2) social values: values belonging to people from the same society and/or social class; and (3) historical values: values originating from an era in history.

Visual language: the components of visual texts (such as a cartoon, photograph, table or graph): how they are framed, the accompanying body text, shading and focal point. Also includes visual features related to a form, e.g. bullet points or logo.

Voice: the individual style of an author that makes their writing unique to them. It includes elements such as detailed personal knowledge and tone.

How to improve your vocabulary

One way to improve your English score is to develop a sophisticated vocabulary. There are many words and terms that high-achieving students automatically know. If you want to achieve high scores like they do, you need to understand and learn to use these words effectively. This is a basic skill that you can work on.

The following is a list of one hundred commonly used words, in alphabetical order, used in media texts. Read through them and ask yourself the following questions:

1 How many words have I read before?
2 How many words can I give explanations/definitions for?
3 How many words can I use confidently in my writing?

While you can always take a dictionary into SACs and exams, you may not find some words and terms that have another, non-literal meaning in your usual dictionary. For example; 'white elephant' is another name for a useless item. It doesn't always mean a white-coloured elephant.

A–Z words in media texts

A	ambivalent, amnesty, ambiguous, amoral, accolades, anomalies
B	bespoke, bipartisan, behemoth
C	conservative, clandestine, convoluted, conducive, catalyst, classic, Cold War
D	draconian, democracy, diplomatic, diverse, dubious, definitive, doldrums
E	empathy, elite, egalitarian, endemic, eponymous, enigma, exodus
F	futile, faux pas, Fat Cat
G	greenie, golden child

H	heinous, heroic, hippie, honeymoon period, hoi polloi, hip pocket
I	insidious, ignoramus, initiative, infamous, immoral, injustice
J	justice, judicious, jargon
K	kamikaze, karma
L	left wing, liberal, lost in limbo
M	mercurial, maligned, mitigating, moral, misogynist, messiah
N	nemesis, nepotism
O	obscene, obtuse, optimistic, orthodox
P	pessimistic, pedantic, prestigious, perennial, paradox, paradigm, polemic, partisan, parochial
Q	quid pro quo, quintessential
R	radical, right wing
S	secular, stigmatise, stereotype, seminal, sympathy, scapegoat
T	tenuous, tree-hugger
U	ubiquitous
V	vox pop, vendetta, vale
W	warmonger, white elephant, wowser
X	xenophobic
Y	yuppie, yellow streak
Z	zeitgeist, Zen

Practice activities

1 Create your own word bank.
Read through 'A-Z words in media texts' and identify any words you don't know Construct a table like below and write definitions and examples using the word(s).

Word	**Definition**	**Example**
'lost in limbo'	Not belonging in any place. Stranded between heaven and hell.	Poor Sarah was lost in limbo after her dog died.

2 Target your language analysis verbs.
Copy the following 'Language analysis verbs chart' and target four in each category

For more language analysis verbs, read Chapter 4.

Language analysis verbs chart

Categories	**Verbs**	**Examples**
Contention	Contends, states, asserts, claims	In her blog, Rose Laurie *contends* that …

Structure	Opens, begins, continues, concludes	Dr Maxwell *concludes* his presentation by inviting his audience to …
How a persuasive technique is used	Emphasises, highlights, demonstrates, suggests, reiterates, signals, provides, uses, employs	The cropped photograph of three chickens cramped into a tiny cage clearly *demonstrates* the 'inhumane conditions' described by Smith.
Impact on audience	Evokes, alienates, positions, appeals, influences, compels, encourages, generates, prompts, arouses	The disturbing photo *causes* readers to feel uncomfortable, *prompting* them to speak out against the 'abused' animals.

Chapter 2

General language analysis – what you need to know

THE TASK
The language analysis question on the SAC and in the exam will ask you *how* the written and visual language is used to attempt to persuade the audience to share the point(s) of view in three or more persuasive texts. A persuasive text may be a photograph, letter, editorial or blog. There will always be at least one visual text for you to analyse.

SAMPLE TASK
'How does the writer use written and visual language to attempt to persuade readers to share his point of view?' [VCAA 2013 exam]

SAMPLE EAL TASK
Part 1
Write a note-form summary of the speech by Mrs Elliot. Your response must be in note form. Do not use complete sentences.

Part 2
Write a piece of prose that explains how language and visual features have been used in the speech by Mrs Elliot to attempt to persuade the audience about three of the main points in the speech. [VCAA 2012 exam]

Four 'big picture' questions

Before you can effectively analyse the written and visual language in texts, you need to understand that language analysis is not just about identifying persuasive techniques. To effectively analyse media texts you need to understand the 'big picture': how the text works as a whole to attempt to persuade the intended or target audience. You need to ask yourself four 'big picture' questions:

1 *How* did this issue arise?
2 *Who* is the author and *what* is their point of view on the issue?
3 *How* does the author try to persuade their audience?
4 *Who* is the target audience and what are they likely to feel and believe, and how may they think or act after reading the text(s)?

These four 'big picture' questions break down into the following 10 general analysis points. Each point is discussed in further detail with examples in this chapter. Persuasive techniques are explained with sample analysis in Chapter 3.

Top 10 analysis points

1 Issue	What issue? Type? Level? Affects whom?
2 Context (background information)	What event happened? Why was the text created? Who created the texts? Are they experts?
3 Form (written/visual)	What is the form? What conventions or features do we expect? E.g. editorials are strongly opinionated. What structure is used? Language?
4 Audience and audience impact, appeals to different emotions	Who is the audience? Can you stereotype them? E.g. parents who are worried about their children's safety on trains. What does author want audience to feel, think or believe about issue? What emotional appeals will connect with them?
5 Purpose	Why has the author written or created a text? E.g. to protest, to agree
6 Contention	What is the contention? What are the arguments or main points to support the contention? Against?
7 Argument structure	What are the main points being presented? In what order? Why?
8 Tone and tonal shift	How does author sound about topic? E.g. angry, passionate, humorous. Does author change tones? Why?
9 Style – language	How would you describe the overall language? E.g. emotive, logical, personal, formal.
10 Style – persuasive techniques	What persuasive techniques are used? How do they position audience? What is the likely impact on audience?

What are issues?

Issues are topics that you can discuss or debate because they have at least two sides to consider and several different points of view people can argue. Media texts are full of topical issues because the public want to discuss and voice their point of view on all sorts of issues, such as those associated with legal rights, social justice, the environment, religion, politics, finance and sports.

Levels and types of issues

Issues can be categorised into different levels: global, national, state, local or belonging to a specific group, e.g. school, local basketball club or community group.

Issues can be categorised into different types: political, gender, sports, religious, economic, medical, moral, environmental, educational and social. An issue usually involves more than one type.

Topical issues	Level	Type
Drugs in sport	Local – global	Ethical, economic, medical, political
Capital punishment	Global	Political, religious, moral, justice
Wearing religious symbols or garments	National	Political, social, moral, religious
Whaling	Global	Environmental, political, cultural

See the end of this chapter for a list of topical issues.

Events

Issues arise from events. For example, the 2007 Tour de France cycle race was an event where leading cyclists were forced to quit the race for cheating by using drugs. The actual event wasn't the issue, but it was the catalyst for ensuing public debates about the complex issue of 'drug use in sport' that still continues today. Different points of view emerged from these debates and these points of view, in turn, produce contentions.

EVENT
↓
ISSUE
↓
DIFFERENT POINT(S) OF VIEW
↓
CONTENTION(S)
↙ ↘
ARGUMENTS FOR ARGUMENTS AGAINST

Point of view (POV) and contention

Issues spark much debate and many different opinions or points of view (POV). Different POVs on the issue 'drug use in sport' regarding the Tour de France include:

- drug use in sport is wrong
- drug use in sport is OK
- drug use in sport is OK under certain conditions.

A contention is the central message that an author wants their intended audience to accept. Contentions are formed from different POVs on an issue. They are more specific than POVs.

Contentions from the above POVs include:

- cycling should be banned from the Olympics because of cheating
- drug cheats in sport should be banned for life
- cycling teams (including doctors and owners), as well as the cyclists, should be penalised for cheating
- the Tour de France should be abandoned because of endemic cheating
- advances in science and technology will always result in drug cheats in sport.

Arguments and main points

Arguments must support an author's contention. An author may have three or more major arguments and main points, or one complicated argument with many main/key points. If an author has only one slim argument, they may find it extremely difficult to convince their audience.

CONTENTION
That drug cheats should be banned for life
↙ ↘

ARGUMENTS FOR	ARGUMENTS AGAINST
• Betrays public	• Life ban is too long
• Sends clear message to athletes	• It's endemic and unstoppable
• Sports stars should be role models	• Different drugs = different penalties
• No funding	• Everybody makes mistakes
• Poor reputation → effects	• Accidental drug-taking?

Context (background information)

The context is the background information to an issue. It may describe the event from which the issue arose. This background information is supplied with texts for analysis. It is usually located in a box after the task description. Always read this carefully as often the form, audience, visual language and the event or reasons why the texts have been written are identified. Knowing this background information helps you contextualise the texts, and can help you identify the contention and stereotype the audience.

See the following example from Section C of the 2012 English exam.

Background information

- The following pages contain the transcript of a speech by Mrs Elliot, a retired teacher–librarian, at the opening of 'Reading: The Future', a forum on reading and literacy-related activities.
- Two slides used by the speaker during her presentation are also shown.
- The audience included teachers, librarians and senior school students from local schools.

The above example provides the following information for you to use in your analysis:

- *Form* is a speech at 'Reading: The Future' at the opening of a forum.
- *Visual language* includes two slides.
- *Audience* includes teachers, librarians and senior school students.
- The speaker/author is a retired teacher–librarian, so has *expertise* with reading and literacy, and can speak with *authority* and confidence.

Media texts

Media texts (print, non-print and multimodal) are persuasive texts because they are topical issues. They try to persuade you about an issue, idea, person or product.

Print texts	Non-print texts	Multimodal
Editorials	Speeches	CD-ROMs
Letters to the editor	Segments from current	DVDs
Blogs, Emails,	affairs	TV ads
Facebook page,	Radio talkback	Ezines
Tweets	Online forums	Websites
Opinion columns	Radio and TV	Documentaries
Essays, transcripts	Interviews	Blogs
Reviews	Chat room	Online media articles
Newsletters	Podcast	Advertisements
Brochures	Oral presentations	Interactive texts
Submissions	Excerpts from online	
Reports	focus and discussion	
Visual texts	groups	
Cartoons		
Tables		
Graphs		
Posters, ads		
Photographs		

Types of exam persuasive texts 2008–2012

According to VCAA you can be asked to write an analysis of three or more different texts. While there will always be at least one visual text, there are different possible combinations of persuasive texts for you to analyse.
Examples are:

- a feature article with a photo plus a response
- a speech with slides (visuals)
- an online opinion piece with an image and another opinion piece embedded in it
- a blog with an important post, photos and responses
- a newsletter with sign and letter in response

Persuasive text forms in 2008–2013 exams

Exam year	Form	Issue	Number of texts	Word count
2008	Newsletter with cartoon	Sports rage	2	704
2009	Opinion piece with embedded text and photo	Digital technology	3	1097
2010	Speech with 2 slides (photos)	Biodiversity	3	939
2011	Blog with 4 posts and 2 photos	Tattoos	7	Blog = 600 Posts = 40–100
2012	Speech with 2 slides (photo and cartoon)	E-reading	3	874
2013	Newsletter with poster and graph	Community garden	3	

See the following diagrams for possible combinations of persuasive texts in a SAC or exam. How you structure your analysis depends on the number of texts you are asked to analyse and the length of these texts. There are three weave structures for writing your analysis: mini weave, semi weave and total weave. See Chapter 4 for detailed information.
sample 1 sample s

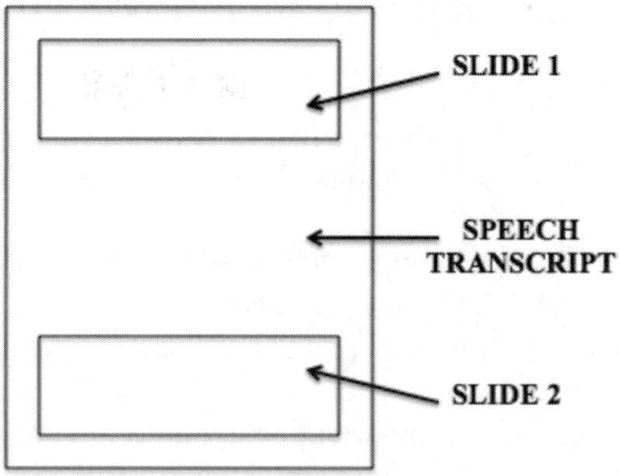

Figure 2.1 Three texts

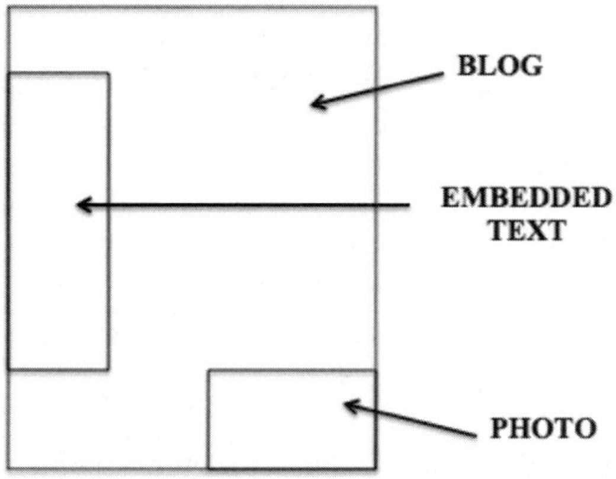

Figure 2.2 Three texts (but we can treat the embedded text as part of the blog)

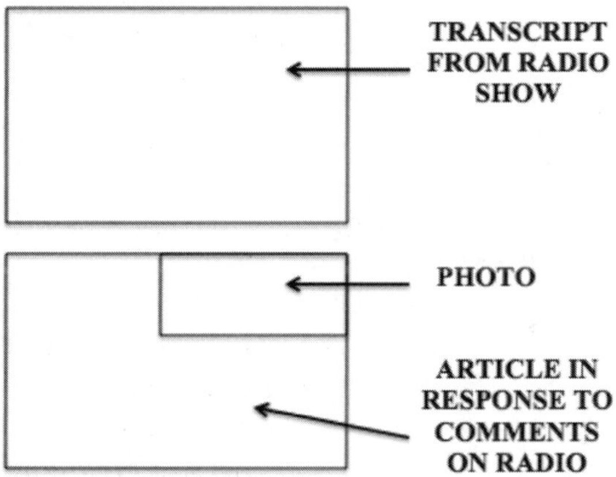

Figure 2.3 Three texts

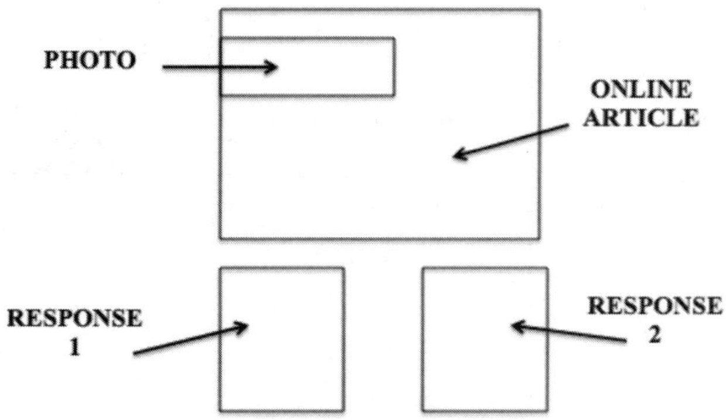

Figure 2.4 Four texts

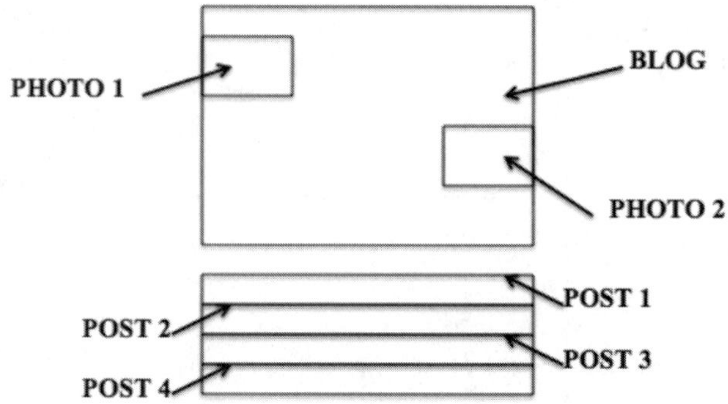

Figure 2.5 Seven texts but we would treat the four posts as one text

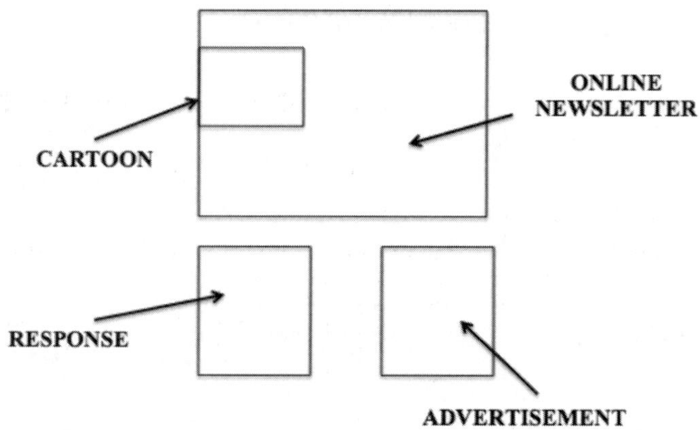

Figure 2.6 Four texts

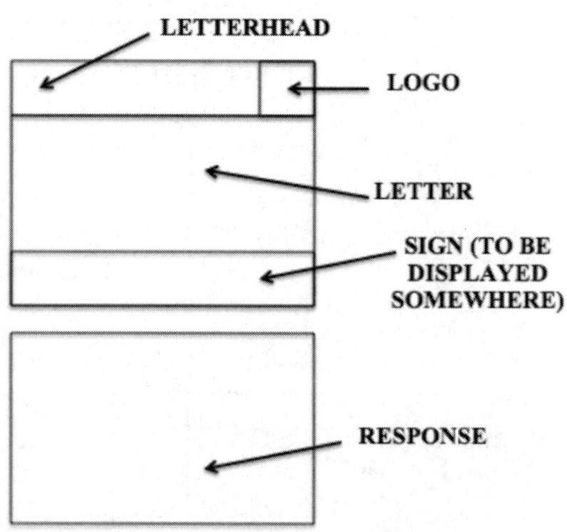

Figure 2.7 Three texts plus letterhead and logo, which are visual features

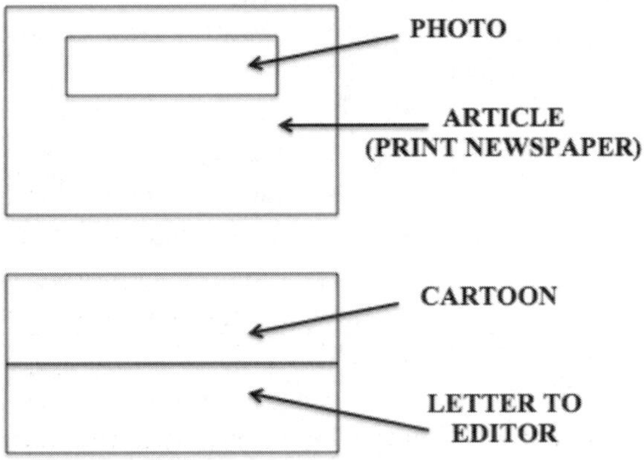

Figure 2.8 Four texts

Forms and features (conventions) of media texts

All forms (text types) of media texts have expected features or conventions. These are the features that audiences expect. Being aware of these expected conventions makes it easier to analyse and compare media texts on an issue and enables you to comment on how they influence argument and position the audience. You also need to know these features when you write your own point-of-view text.

Form	Features
Editorial	• Briefly describes event and development of issue. • Uses headline, an authoritative tone and inclusive language e.g. ‘we’ and ‘our’. Does not use ‘I’. • Presents key arguments and evidence on both sides. • Formal structure and language. Makes confident recommendations. Uses strong language. • Name of author not given – usually a senior writer. • No visuals. Can include a call to action.
Article	• Short, catchy headline (e.g. alliteration). • Visual with caption and/or speech bubble. • 1st para = summary of incident/event. 2nd + 3rd paragraphs = Who? What? Where? When? Why? + evidence in body. • Often uses single sentence paragraphs. • Last sentence = strong conclusion or indicates follow-up.

Letter/email to editor	• Supports or challenges point-of-view voiced in publication. May include a different viewpoint entirely. • States contention and issue clearly. • Personal style –'I', 'my' and anecdotal evidence. • Uses inclusive language, 'we', 'our', 'us'. • Less formal than article or editorial. • May include emotive language and/or personal attacks, humour.
Essay/opinion piece/newsletter	• Clear argument. • Each paragraph adds key points. • Compares and contrasts arguments. Uses facts. • May be written in 1st or 3rd person, include anecdotal evidence, personal content, view, tone and voice. • May include visual language.
Report/submission	• Explains different points of view on issue. Uses objective, formal language, past tense of verbs and appropriate technical jargon. • Presents information clearly and logically. • Bullet points, headings and subheadings may be used. • General conclusion can be reached. • Recommendations and judgements may be made.
Speech	• Engaging introduction, e.g. statistic, anecdote. Formal introduction/salutation. Point of view stated clearly. • Includes inclusive language, repetition, clear signposts. • Has logical structure. May include visual language, multimedia and audience interaction. • Strong conclusion usually includes a call to action.
Blog entry	• Supports, challenges or presents new point-of-view on issue. 1st person, anecdotal evidence. • May include inclusive language, jargon and visual language. Less formal than article or editorial. • Invites 'posts' (responses) from readers/followers.
Cartoon	Complements contention and/or argument in an accompanying text. Uses humour. Adds evidence or illustrates related aspects of the issue. May include caption or speech bubble (body text).

Photograph	Complements contention and/or argument in an accompanying text. Adds information, evidence or illustrates related aspect of issue. May present emotional content. Framed carefully to position audience to respond in certain way. Often includes a caption.
Radio item news	30–60 seconds per item. Who, what, when and where are stated at start. 'Why' may not be dealt with. May include sound grabs (e.g. live quote).
Radio interviews	Short, e.g. five questions unless a featured interview. May be in studio or in field. Also SFX, sound clips.
Radio talkback	• Introduction to program, number, self and topic by host or shock jock. • 30–60 second period for caller to state point of view. • Host may debate with caller.
TV news or current affairs items/segments/ interviews	• SFX + titles on screen may be used as introduction. • Related visual in background. • May include live or re-enacted footage, interview. • Sometimes includes newsreader's comments. Non-verbal language, e.g. gestures and facial expressions.
Tweet	• Uses abbreviated and informal language e.g. LOL • Written concisely

Audience and audience impact

The audience is who reads, listens to and/or views a text. Knowing the intended or target audience is extremely important for an author as they must use language, persuasive techniques and tone that enable them to connect with their audience in order to appeal to their emotions.

When you analyse media texts you need to:

1. identify your target audience
2. stereotype the target audience (in your head)
3. comment on the likely impact the persuasive techniques used will have on target audience.

Target audiences

Examples of target audiences are:

- wage earners
- parents
- environmentalists
- teenagers
- public transport users
- teachers
- shop owners
- residents
- cricket fans
- chess players

- movie goers
- rate payers
- travellers
- senior citizen

Stereotyping the audience
Authors try to stereotype their audience so that they can anticipate how they may feel about an issue and what they might think, feel or do in response to a particular issue. They do this by researching the following:

- gender
- age range
- general likes and dislikes
- likely beliefs about politics
- likely fears and frustrations
- social and cultural values.

When you stereotype the target audience you need to:

1 Put yourself in their shoes and try to identify what emotions they might feel about certain issues and why e.g. parents feeling guilty if their child spends too much time gaming.

2 Decide how they may be likely to be influenced by author's argument or certain appeal i.e. anticipate what they might think, feel and how they may act about an issue and think which persuasive techniques would enable an author to position them to agree with their argument.

Likely audience impact
A result of the persuasive technique of a personal anecdote may be to, e.g., increase the target audience's frustration with their local council, resulting in letters to the council.

Example of analysis of a media text
Text: Cyberbullying – the truth

Audience: Parents of young children.

Stereotype: They will usually be concerned, even fearful, for their children's health and safety. They want to be responsible parents.

Persuasive techniques: An article by Dr Kinnear, an expert in cyberbullying,

where he presents evidence about the harmful effects of cyberbullying and offers practical advice.

Likely impact: The article may scare or shock parents and encourage them to accept and implement the advice given by Dr Kinnear, in order to be responsible parents.

Remember that the audience for language analysis is usually included in the **background information.**

Target audience	**Issue**	**How stereotype audience might feel**	**Likely impact**
Wage earners	Tax increase	Frustrated with way government uses taxed income	Generate complaints
Environmentalists	All whaling must stop.	Angry at /passionate about inhumane treatment of whales	Join movement, sign petition
Teenagers	P Plate drivers increase in hours	Unfairly treated, particularly P Platers in country. Victimised.	Complain to state government, protest via social media
Public transport users	Increase in cost of fines	Thinks is justice if it means they are no longer subsidising fare evaders. Likely to agree	Happy if fare evaders are being caught.

Purpose

The purpose is why a text is created. All authors of media texts aim to persuade their audience to accept their point of view on an issue, but they may do this in different ways. They might be responding to a previous article, recommending an alternative way, attacking another person or refuting an accusation. It is important to identify these and say *how* they might help persuade.

Examples of different purposes are:

- attack
- refute
- recommend
- comment on
- challenge a stance on an issue
- respond or address a stance
- criticise
- satirise
- protest
- inform.

Tone

Tone is the attitude of an author or creator towards the issue they are discussing. It is the way a written text would sound if it is read aloud. Tone refers to the mood of a visual text, e.g. humorous, friendly or aggressive. The language used in a written text conveys the tone. Tone is part of an author's style and needs to suit the purpose and audience. Visual features in a written text, e.g. logo and letterhead, help to create tone.

Tonal shift

Sometimes an author will use more than one tone in a text. When the tone changes it is called a tonal shift. For example, a psychologist giving a speech to parents and teenagers about the harmful effects of videogaming may begin using a friendly tone in order to connect with their audience. However, as they list statistics about the potential dangers of videogaming, their tone may become authoritative and appeal to the audience's sense of fear about their children's safety.

An author may use a range of tones in their text and there may be more than one tonal shift. While there are many words to describe tone, students can sometimes find it difficult to identify and analyse tone in written texts. In order to identify tones you need to read the text as a whole and ask questions like:

- Does the writer sound positive? E.g. upbeat, optimistic, cheerful tone
- Is writer trying to scare or warn? E.g. alarmed, ominous (warning) tone
- Is writer an expert? E.g. authoritative, confident, matter-of-fact tone.

For more questions and examples of tone, see Tone chart in Chapter 4.

Language style

Style is an author's individual stamp on a text – the thing that makes an author's writing different from other writing on the same issue. It is an overall description. An author's language style must suit the purpose and intended audience, otherwise the text will not work – it will not persuade the target audience to agree with author's point of view.

Language style is deliberately chosen to manipulate the audience; e.g. formal styles create an impression of authority. There are different ways to analyse style. Some students write about an overall style as in examples 1 and 2.

Example 1

'Councillor Felicity O'Brien addresses her audience informally, drawing them into the group that must face the current problem of litter in the community.'

Example 2

'Dr Ellen McQueen's use of formal style and extensive research findings establishes her authority about gaming addiction to her audience of parents.'

When writing an analysis, some students find identifying the overall writing style difficult and therefore choose to comment on the three main persuasive techniques or points, including visual language used, instead – see examples 3 and 4.

Example 3

'Councillor Felicity O'Brien uses a combination of visual language, emotive appeals and inclusive language in a bid to convince the local community that the new litter tax is necessary.'

Example 4

'Dr Ellen McQueen combines an ominous tone with facts and slides of worrying statistics to warn her audience of parents that addiction to gaming is detrimental to their children's mental and physical development.'

Examples of language style words are:

- convoluted
- formal
- informal
- cynical
- matter-of-fact
- humorous
- logical
- old-fashioned
- concise or succinct
- poetic
- straightforward
- factual
- cogent.

How persuasive texts are structured

How persuasive texts structure arguments about an issue is both deliberate and very important. Authors of persuasive texts build their case using arguments to support their contention and convince the target audience to agree with their point of view. They use signposts, connectives, link words, lexical chains and visual language features to make their arguments logical and to reinforce points so that the target audience can easily comprehend their message.

It is important in your analysis that you comment on how the structure of the text positions the target audience and its likely impact. Knowing the ten argument essentials below will help you analyse the structure and also help you structure your own arguments when you write a point-of-view text.

Ten argument essentials

1. The opening grabs attention and sets up expectations.
2. The contention is clearly stated with the main points briefly mentioned.
3. The main points are elaborated and support the contention.
4. Factual evidence is used to support the main points.
5. Persuasive language and techniques are used throughout text.
6. Connectives, signposts and linking are used to orientate audience.
7. The main opposing argument is rebutted.
8. The language suits the target audience and the chosen form.
9. Visual language and features are used to reinforce points.
10. There is a strong conclusion. It may state how the audience is expected to act i.e. call to action.

Signposts

Signposts are words and phrases that clarify points and inform the reader what to expect.

Here are some examples:

- 'There are three ways to …'; 'First, …', 'second, …', 'third, …'
- 'It follows logically that … '
- 'There are three ways of addressing this problem and they are … '
- 'I will begin with …'
- 'Finally … '
- 'While some people may say [rebut], however … '

Link words

Examples of link words are 'furthermore', 'similarly', 'therefore', 'however', 'but', 'unlike', 'although', 'despite'.

Lexical chains

Lexical chains are patterns that connect words in a text. They include:

- *repetition*: repeated words in text, possibly from headline or title.
- *synonyms*: words that have similar meanings, but may vary in word strength, e.g. 'society', 'public', 'community', 'Australians'.
- *hyponyms*: words that can be expressed by more general words – e.g. 'tiger', 'lion' and 'elephant' are all hyponyms of 'animal'.
- *cross references*: links to the title, topic, key points, and so on.
- *connectives*: see Chapter 4 for a chart of words used as connectives.

Note-form summary (EAL)

A note-form summary is a brief outline of information presented in a text. It contains the main points required on a topic presented in logical order and is a useful tool for *all* students for understanding an issue. You may choose to divide your summary into a chart or columns, or present it in another way. EAL students need to be able to write a note-form summary, using symbols, on the persuasive text in Task 1 of the exam.

Eight tips for note-form summaries

1 Read/view text carefully.
2 Identify the issue and write it as a main heading.
3 Identify the contention and write it as a subheading.
4 List arguments (the main points) for and against the contention taken from the text.
5 Always write in point form – never use full sentences.
6 Write quotes. Use ellipses (…) when you omit words.
7 Use abbreviations, arrows and symbols.
8 Set notes out clearly.

Note-form conventions		**Accepted symbols**	
b/w	between	&	and
e.g.	for example	=	equals, same as
vs	versus, against	+	adds to, complements
b/c	because	–	lessens, reduces,
re	about, concerning	>	greater than
cf	compare with, contrast	<	less than
w	with	$	money
		*	important
		**	really important
		??	not sure, undecided
		Use arrows to show how points are linked: ➔ 🡅 🡇 🡧 🡮	

Note-form summary example

Reading: The Future [VCAA 2012 exam]
Mrs E (retired teacher + librarian)
F = speech. A = teachers, librarians, students
🡇
ebooks (technology)

+ve 🡄 good + bad (probs) ➔ **-ve**

+ve
- < $
- instant borrowing
- < weight to carry (visual)

-ve
- view ~~read~~
- no imagination
- > screen hrs = unhealthy

- △ brightness + font size
- video + animation
- edictionary = useful

- no 2nd hand stores
- ~~permanent~~ (visual)

'lost' things
↓
cyber disaster → no ebooks
share + lend books
↑gap b/w rich & poor
imagination??
↓
WARNING
ebooks = good
BUT
don't forget

Practice activities

1 Assume that you are a parent in favour of mobile phones at school and complete the following issue map. You will need to include your POV, contention and four arguments or main points to support your contention.

Issue map

Event	Mobile phones stolen at school.	
Issue	Mobile phones	
POV	**Against** From principal – no mobile phones	**For**
Contention	That mobile phones be banned from school	
Arguments/ main points (4)	• School's insurance policy doesn't cover stolen phones. • Phones distract students in class. • Students take embarrassing photos at school and post them on Facebook, damaging school's reputation. • They are not necessary for learning as students have government-supplied tablets.	

2 Construct and complete other issue maps using the topical issues list at the end of this chapter.
3 Read 'Your say' (below) and for each email identify the issue, contention, purpose, tone, language style and any persuasive techniques.

Your say

Poison pokies
Gambling addiction is the biggest problem in this state and the worst addicted to poker machines is the state government. If and when the government reduces its reliance on taxation, we might see some changes for the better health. What are the odds on that?
Rose Larkin, Bentwood

Gownlow winner
My 3–2–1 votes were one for Janie, the blonde in the tight red dress; two for Ellie, the blonde in the tight blue dress with the thigh split, and three for Lulu in the tight orange backless dress with the thigh split. A special nod to veteran Binny who wore a nude gown that was sooo tight that you couldn't tell flesh from dress. BTW Who won Brownlow medal?
Ned Worsnop, Parktone

Dangerous dog owners
Fatal dog attacks like the one that killed Ayen Choi in Aug, 2011 should not be allowed to happen again. Pit bull terriers are required to be leashed and muzzled at all times while outside in a public place. It's the law. We need greater penalties for owners, who are just as dangerous.
Dr Carrie Brown, Crenwick

Anthem angst
It looks bad when cricket players line up for the national anthem and hardly one player moves his lips. I'm not asking for an *X Factor* performance. Just sing it with respect or don't sing it all – it's embarrassing.
Izzy Goodnight, Munji North

Grand Prix pot holes
So, the Phillip Island access road opens just in time for the Grand Prix. God knows how much money it cost. There are 50 potholes on the highway from McKenzie Rd on the mainland to the Grand Prix track. That's only a distance of 25 km. There's no point putting up road safety billboards for motorcyclists on the highway. They are too busy weaving around potholes in the road to notice. Does the government want more road deaths?
Fergus Campbell, Surf Beach

Get serious about smokers
Why can't we ban smoking? Tobacco kills more people than the combined death toll from road accidents, illicit drugs, AIDS, diabetes, murder and skin cancer. Almost any smoking exposure is harmful. Smokers are 32% more likely to end up in hospitals than non-smokers. Absenteeism and non-productive time at work is 70% higher for smokers. They lose on average one hour of productive time per day. Smokers retire earlier. Smoking is socially unacceptable. Let's get serious and cut off the access. Smoking shouldn't be criminalised because smokers need all the help they can get. We should make the commercial sale of tobacco illegal. Let's do it!
Greg Kinnear, Melbourne

Possum magic?
What are Leadbeater's possums and why do we have to save them? Why is hard-earned taxpayers' money spent on stinky, noisy, furry vermin? Why are possums a protected species? They destroy property and sleep. Last summer a nest of possums ate through the roof of my holiday house and some electrical wiring. They cost me $9000. When I called the possum catcher he laughed and told me that I could borrow his cages for free. Apparently when you trap a possum you can release it 50 metres away. What a joke! The only good possum is a flat one.
Al Rickson, Moortown

4 Stereotype the following three examples of target audience and write how they would feel and the likely impact on them of the issue of a 15% increase in movie tickets:
- teenagers
- movie goers
- senior citizens.

Consider the following when stereotyping: gender, age range, general likes and dislikes, likely fears and frustrations, social and cultural values.

5 Choose one of the target audience from Question 4 and write a letter or email to the editor giving your opinion on the issue.

6 Research newspapers (print and online) and select three different media texts on a topical issue:
(a) Read and answer the four 'big picture' questions.
(b) Complete a note-form summary.
(c) Adapt and complete a language analysis overview using the chart at the end of Chapter 3.

7 Read the background information from 2009 exam (below) and then answer the following questions:
(a) What form is the text?
(b) Who is the likely audience?
(c) What is the title of the text?
(d) What was it written in response to?

Background information [Section C, 2009 VCAA English exam]

The following opinion piece appeared in *Ctrl Alt,* an online journal. It was posted earlier this year in response to the increasing debate about the impact of digital technology.

Topical issues list

- Abortion
- Anti-terrorist precautions
- Asylum seekers
- Australian republic
- Bike paths
- Binge-drinking
- Capital punishment
- Casual racism
- CCTV cameras
- Child beauty pageants
- Deforestation
- Depression
- Desalination plants
- Drugs in sport
- Duck shooting
- Euthanasia: involuntary or voluntary
- Extended P plate driver time
- Equal pay for tennis players
- Freedom of speech
- Gay marriage
- Global warming
- Graffiti
- Helmets in sport
- Hoon drivers
- Live shark de-finning
- Logging
- Match-fixing in sport
- Organ donation
- PTSD
- Public transport
- Racial vilification
- Renewable energy
- Restricted dog breeds
- Shark culling
- Teenage gambling
- Whaling

The above list is very general. If you are writing a persuasive text on any of the above you need to:
1 Narrow your focus e.g. Organ donation in Victoria
2 Frame it as a contention e.g. That Victorians need to be better informed about organ donation.

3 List key points for and against your contention, e.g.

FOR	AGAINST
Current organ donation is low	Organs taken from living patients
Dispel myths i.e. not 'brain dead'	
Altruistic act	
One person can save many lives	
Can always change your mind	

Note: Your issue must be one currently debated in Australian media, an issue that has been featured in the Australian media after 30 September of the previous year.

Chapter 3

Persuasive strategies – language and techniques

Authors of media texts always try to persuade their target audience to agree with their point of view. They try to position their audience to think, believe or act in a certain way. To achieve this, authors use a range of strategies including different forms, persuasive written and visual language, techniques and structured arguments.

It's not enough to just identify persuasive techniques and language in your analysis (labelling) – you need to focus on *how* an author uses persuasive techniques and language to strengthen their argument and position their target audience or reader, as well as their likely impact.

Persuasive strategies

Language and technique	**How it persuades**
Active voice When the subject of a sentence does the action, the verb is active, e.g. 'Terrorist acts strike fear in the hearts of many citizens.'	Creates immediacy and a sense of urgency about the matter.
Sample analysis McQueen begins her article with 'Terrorist acts strike fear' using an active voice that immediately creates a sense of urgency in her reader.	
Adjectives Describing words, usually used to describe noun, e.g. 'precious', 'rare'. Comparatives, e.g. 'more precious', and superlatives, e.g. 'most precious'.	Adds emphasis, helps create a mental image.
Sample analysis Mrs Elliot appeals to her audience's nostalgia through her carefully placed adjectives, 'precious' and 'rare', which highlight the craftsmanship associated with the creation of a book.	
Alliteration Repetition of consonant sound, at start of words, e.g. 'Happy hawk's successful hunt'.	Grabs attention and highlights the key words related to issue. Often in headlines. Combines with other techniques, e.g. puns and visuals to give text extra meaning.

<table>
<tr><td colspan="2">Sample analysis
The headline, 'Happy hawk's successful hunt' establishes an upbeat tone from the outset of her article.</td></tr>
<tr><td>Analogy
Comparison or partial comparison between two items, e.g. there is an analogy between a heart and a pump.</td><td>A comparison that can create a positive or negative image in reader's mind.</td></tr>
<tr><td colspan="2">Sample analysis
By using the analogy, 'heart of the team' when referring to Simpson, Coach Taylor impresses upon his audience the essential and important value of Simpson, which may encourage them to do more to retain the player's services.</td></tr>
<tr><td>Anecdote
A brief story – personal or someone else's, e.g. 'Last week I was caught by a ticket inspector on a train without a ticket'.</td><td>Connects and engages readers, personalises a text and can have emotional appeal. Can set up a character, then position the reader to accept or reject that character.</td></tr>
<tr><td colspan="2">Sample analysis
Coach Sam opens his column with an anecdote in italics about eight-year-old 'distraught' Emily, whose 'dad yelled at her' for failing to 'save the game', undermining the credibility of 'aggressive' spectators and provoking readers to respond with protests against such treatment of a child.</td></tr>
<tr><td>Appeals
Authority, common sense, family values, fear and insecurity, hip pocket, justice, logic, patriotism, tradition, self-preservation</td><td>Targets audience's emotions and/or values and attitudes. Can manipulate audience to pay attention to issue by evoking an emotional response.</td></tr>
<tr><td colspan="2">Sample analysis – see the following section in this chapter for more details about appeals and sample sentences for analyses.</td></tr>
<tr><td>Association
Words that create meanings beyond the literal meaning of the word, e.g. 'unattractive', 'pleasing', 'honest', 'professional'.</td><td>Suggests or influences audience's response, often subconsciously, with further implied meanings associated with the word.</td></tr>
<tr><td colspan="2">Sample analysis
The increasingly unattractive image of people with ill-planned tattoos is magnified as Day associates them with 'newsreaders, sitcom stars and upmarket shoppers'.</td></tr>
</table>

<table>
<tr><td>Bias
Favouring one side in presentation of opinion, e.g. an article written about hundreds of chickens being freed by activists, by an author who is a member of Australians for Animal Rights (AAR).</td><td>Can influence reader by presenting only one side of an argument.
Can undermine the argument by presenting too much bias.</td></tr>
<tr><td colspan="2">Sample analysis
Smith’s inherent bias sees her label fellow AAR members as ‘compassionate’ for their act in ‘liberating’ chickens, which may alienate readers who are not members of this group.</td></tr>
<tr><td>Cliché
An overused expression, often colloquial, familiar to audience, e.g. ‘the bottom line’ and ‘it’s not what you know but who you know’.</td><td>Familiar to audience and a shortcut to illustrate meaning. Can be humorous. Often used in headlines. Can position the audience to accept an idea because they are familiar with it, and offer a shortcut to convey meaning.</td></tr>
<tr><td colspan="2">Sample analysis
Williams’s use of clichés throughout his piece is likely to resonate with his audience of businesspeople who easily understand the meanings associated with the ‘bottom line’.</td></tr>
<tr><td>Colourful language
Words that are heightened and full of interest, e.g. bad = disgraceful, unfair, irresponsible, detrimental</td><td>Catches the audience’s interest, paints a memorable image and can evoke emotion. Can position the audience to adopt a strong positive or negative view on topic.</td></tr>
<tr><td colspan="2">Sample analysis
McQueen’s description of the ‘blistering hot’ conditions at the tennis is likely to provoke outrage from her readers towards the organisers, who refuse to provide free drinking water.</td></tr>
<tr><td>Connotations and loaded words
Meanings associated with or implied by words. They are not literal or meanings from the dictionary, e.g. ‘comrades’, ‘greenies’, ‘the sisterhood is strong here’, ‘slacker’.</td><td>Associated meanings and implications of words can evoke existing emotions and attitudes of audience and manipulate their thinking to accept or reject an idea, person, etc. Discredits people by association. Can be a shorthand way of discrediting someone. Usually assumes audience agreement.</td></tr>
</table>

<table>
<tr><td colspan="2">Sample analysis
Derwent's loaded comment about 'the sisterhood being strong here' may alienate the female members of his audience with its negative connotation and, in turn, prompt complaints of misogyny.</td></tr>
<tr><td>Colloquial language
Words and phrases that are informal, popular and in current usage. Unlike slang, they are more widely known, e.g. 'cool'.</td><td>Can connect with audience and work as inclusive language does. Can also disconnect with or exclude members of audience who do not understand colloquialism.</td></tr>
<tr><td colspan="2">Sample analysis
Cook's assurance that the new device is 'cool' appeals to the Gen Y members of her audience who are likely to Google the device and find out more.</td></tr>
<tr><td>Emotive language
Deliberate use of strong language to evoke emotions of audience, e.g. 'a heartless proposition to cruelly evict these citizens'.</td><td>Audience is positioned to react very emotionally and to agree with author's point of view before any evidence is presented.</td></tr>
<tr><td colspan="2">Sample analysis
Messil emotively describes the proposition as 'heartless' and 'cruel[ly]', inviting her reader's to share her sense of compassion.</td></tr>
<tr><td>Evidence
Facts, statistics, statements and information to provide proof and support viewpoint e.g. '35% loss of mangroves, 40% of forests and 50% of wetlands'.</td><td>Positions audience to accept argument as it adds credibility (weight) and appears objective and reliable.
Note: Always check the source!</td></tr>
<tr><td colspan="2">Sample analysis
Professor Feng introduces alarming statistics of loss, such as '35% of mangroves, 40% of forests and 50% of wetlands', which are likely to shock his audience.</td></tr>
<tr><td>Exaggeration (hyperbole)
Offers extreme view of situation for dramatic effect, e.g. 'I love it'. Hyperbole can also be affected by a simile.</td><td>Dramatic effect reinforces point and gains attention. Can elicit strong and/or emotional response from audience. Can also be humorous. Often used in headlines.</td></tr>
<tr><td colspan="2">Sample analysis
'It's fun' and 'it's exciting' are examples of hyperbole that develop her stance as an understanding and dedicated speaker in the eyes of the audience.</td></tr>
<tr><td>Expert opinion
Use of titles and expertise, e.g. 'Dr Alexander Tulloch of the Royal South Hospital, stated that … '</td><td>Adds credibility to argument or evidence presented and positions the audience to accept the argument or evidence as they assume expertise</td></tr>
</table>

<table>
<tr><td></td><td>associated with title. Note: Check that the qualifications and expertise are genuine and relevant!</td></tr>
<tr><td colspan="2">Sample analysis
The fact that Dr Tulloch has worked in the cardiac unit at Royal South Hospital for 20 years influences the reader to accept his observations of patients as they would probably regard him as an expert.</td></tr>
<tr><td>Figurative language
Alliteration: see earlier in this table.
Simile: comparison of two objects, e.g. ‘She’s like a moral compass’.
Metaphor: a stronger comparison of two objects, e.g. ‘Dr Jiang is the moral compass of the Health Party’.
Personification: attributing human characteristics to inanimate objects, e.g. ‘My computer died’.</td><td>Presents information in a humorous or memorable way by creating visual and auditory images. Can connect with audience’s experience of feelings about an issue.</td></tr>
<tr><td colspan="2">Sample analysis
Opening with, ‘When did your computer last die?’, Kevinson quickly signals to his target audience his humorous tone and understanding of technology problems.</td></tr>
<tr><td>Formal language
Adheres to standard Australian English. More elaborate and precise than informal language. Formal grammar and tone. No contractions and only accepted abbreviations are used.</td><td>Can make the text sound more authoritative, more credible and lend weight to argument. If not suited to target audience, formal language can be exclusive and alienate the audience.</td></tr>
<tr><td colspan="2">Sample analysis
Opening with the salutation, ‘Ladies and gentlemen’, Lee immediately asserts the formality not only of his presentation but of the conference as a whole.</td></tr>
<tr><td>Generalisation
A sweeping statement that suggests that what’s true for some is true for all people in that particular group, e.g. ‘teachers’ or ‘teenagers’. Sometimes begins with ‘all’ or ‘every’, e.g. ‘Every concerned individual’.</td><td>Appeals to reader’s general sense or may select prevailing prejudices and seeks to exclude those who do not agree.</td></tr>
<tr><td colspan="2">Sample analysis
Grenfell seeks to undermine the reader’s respect for ‘teachers’ by comparing their number of annual holidays with those of ‘other workers’.</td></tr>
</table>

<table>
<tr><td>Inclusive language
Words that include the audience in the same group as the author, e.g. ‘we’, ‘our’, ‘us’.</td><td>The reader is positioned to feel part of the group and inclined to agree as they may feel excluded if they don’t agree.</td></tr>
<tr><td colspan="2">Sample analysis
Voxi’s constant use of ‘we’ and ‘our’ together with a confident tone and positive ‘spin’ on all aspects of digital technology are likely to appeal to her ‘digital savvy’ readers, who are flattered to see themselves as heading for the 22nd century of ‘spirited optimism’.</td></tr>
<tr><td>Informal language
Includes slang, colloquialism, jargon and some visual features, e.g. ‘helpful NOT!!!’.
Slang is language specific to a particular country or region, e.g. ‘bogan’.
For ‘colloquial language’, see earlier in this chart; for ‘jargon’, see later.</td><td>Can establish a connection with the audience, appear friendly and conversational. Slang appeals to the sense of identity.
Likely to alienate audience if overused or audience doesn’t understand terms.</td></tr>
<tr><td colspan="2">Sample analysis
TV critic Clarice Hannibal’s use of popular slang terms such as ‘bogan’, ‘povvo’ and ‘random’ appeals to her teenage audience who are likely to watch Chris Lilley’s latest production.</td></tr>
<tr><td>Irony
When the writer says one thing, but their meaning is the opposite.</td><td>Can appeal to audience’s sense of humour or intellect by denigrating or mocking subject.</td></tr>
<tr><td colspan="2">Sample analysis
The title of the blog entry, ‘The Power of Ink’, is ironic as Day argues that the tattoo has lost its ‘power’ to commonality.</td></tr>
<tr><td>Jargon
Language used for specific audiences like sports groups, computer users, people who do specialised work, and members of subcultures e.g. ‘twitter-speak’, ‘hashtag’, ‘block’, ‘tweet’.</td><td>Acts as inclusive language for members of specific audience. Can give author authority and impress audience.
Can alienate or exclude audience members who do not understand.</td></tr>
<tr><td colspan="2">Sample analysis
Her constant use of twitter jargon such as ‘block’ and ‘tweet’ may, however, alienate readers who are not ‘twitter savvy’.</td></tr>
<tr><td>Personal attack
An attack on a person that may or may not be connected to an issue. Attempts to discredit the person as</td><td>Can place doubt in the reader’s mind about a person’s character which, in turn, can influence whether or not the reader accepts the author’s stance or</td></tr>
</table>

<table>
<tr><td>unreliable, e.g. 'Ms Blackburn is a dole-bludging hippie'.</td><td>argument – regardless of lack of evidence. May offend some members of audience and detract from the argument.
Note: Check for evidence or facts to substantiate attacks.</td></tr>
<tr><td colspan="2">*Sample analysis*
By attacking Ms Blackburn and calling her a 'dole-bludging hippie', Greenwood seeks to create doubt in the reader's mind about Blackburn's character and, by extension, her idea for a community recycling tax.</td></tr>
<tr><td>**Graphic imagery**
Words that can paint a strong image. May be highly emotive, e.g. 'bodies of bomb victims scattered on the road'.</td><td>Creates strong images in minds of audience. Can appeal to reader's sense of justice or injustice, and provoke a strongly emotive reaction.</td></tr>
<tr><td colspan="2">*Sample analysis*
The graphic description of 'bodies of bomb victims' being 'scattered on the road' is likely to provoke an emotional reaction from readers, who will be saddened by the loss of innocent lives and alarmed by terrorist acts.</td></tr>
<tr><td>**Pun**
Play on words. Often used in headlines.</td><td>Designed to create humour, amuse the reader, and appeal to the intellect and humour of the reader.</td></tr>
<tr><td colspan="2">*Sample analysis*
The title of Smith's article, *Chickens Range Free*, is a pun on 'free range chickens' – it highlights to the reader that now the chickens have been 'liberated' and are now 'range free'.</td></tr>
<tr><td>**Rhetorical question**
A dramatic question that doesn't require an answer because the answer is embedded in the question, or the answer is already understood, e.g. 'Do patients need to die before the government acts?' It can also signal a tonal shift.</td><td>A powerful strategy that can position audience so that to disagree would be to reject a point that clearly commands agreement.</td></tr>
<tr><td colspan="2">*Sample analysis*
There is a strong tonal shift brought about by the question, 'So what's there to worry about?'</td></tr>
<tr><td>**Repetition**
Repeated words, phrases, ideas, images and sentence patterns.</td><td>Used to emphasise a point and reinforce argument and ensure that audience remembers point.</td></tr>
<tr><td colspan="2">*Sample analysis*
Through his repetition of the positive adjectives, 'fair' and 'just', Merman seeks to coerce the reader into believing that voting for Amalgam Party is the responsible thing to do.</td></tr>
</table>

Appeals

Appeals can be visual or written and are designed to provoke an emotional response from the target audience. They can be a very powerful tool of persuasion as they play on people's values, beliefs, loyalties and emotions which, in turn, shape their opinions. An author uses 'appeals' to target specific emotions or values of their target audience in order to manipulate or position them into thinking a certain way, believing something or prompting them to act in a certain way.

When you analyse a text you need to identify:

1. the types of emotional appeals that have been included
2. the likely impact of an appeal on the target audience, i.e. how they might influence the audience to think, believe, say or act about the issue.

Note: Don't write, 'Brantham *makes* his audience feel sad about the …' Use more sophisticated verbs like 'positions', 'encourages', 'elicits' when describing appeals and likely audience impact. See chapter 4 for more audience impact verbs.

Types of appeals

- Fear
- Insecurity
- Sense of guilt
- Compassion
- Group loyalty
- Logic or common sense
- Sense of fairness
- Justice
- 'Coolness'
- Pride
- Hip pocket (financial)
- Patriotism
- National identity
- Moral values
- Humanitarian instincts
- Parental responsibility
- Social responsibility
- Self-interest
- Tradition
- Community interest

Likely impact of an appeal on the audience

1. Stereotype the audience, e.g. responsible parents, people with home loans, people who are concerned about the environment, sports fans, people who use public transport.
2. Try to think how the target audience might feel about an issue.
3. Determine how the appeal might influence the audience to think, believe, say or act about the issue. Read the following examples carefully.

Example 1

'This new government initiative will see more taxpayers' hard-earned dollars go down the drain.'

Audience: Taxpayers

Stereotype audience: feel frustrated that they are constantly losing money to government.

Appeal: financial – hip pocket

Likely impact: further increase in frustration with government, possibly resulting in letter writing, disillusionment and not voting for the present government.

Sample analysis: Appealing to tax payers' hip pocket, McQueen highlights the 'new government initiative' which provokes further frustration with the government from the reader.

Example 2

'It's not a case of if there will be a terrorist attack in Australia, but when.'
Ged Griffin, Victorian Police Counter Terrorism Force.

Audience: Australian citizens

Stereotype audience: feel that Australia is so far away it's safe, or are concerned about possible terrorist attacks

Appeal: fear for safety, or shock

Likely impact: adhere to new anti-terrorist measures, become more aware, demand more safety measures

Sample analysis: McQueen's quote from expert, Ged Griffin from Victorian Police Counter Terrorism Force, may shock readers who feel that Australia is so far away from terrorist zones.

Example 3

'More than 30% of school children are overweight.'

Audience: parents

Stereotype audience: parents are always concerned about their children's health and being responsible parents

Appeal: parental responsibility and guilt

Likely impact: prompt action about their children's current diet or investigation of healthier food choices

Sample analysis: The alarming statistic that '30% of school children are overweight' arouses feelings of parental responsibility and guilt as the audience is compelled to review their own situation.

Visual language

Visual language can have a powerful impact on an audience and be very persuasive. Cartoonist for *The Age*, Mick Connolly, describes drawing as 'a shortcut to an idea' and says that a cartoonist needs to 'take time to understand the subject, know what you want to say and have an opinion, then look for a joke or an unexpected way to say it'.

Visual language forms and features

Different forms of visual texts include cartoons, photographs, tables, graphs, community posters, advertisements, stills from a TV news report and videoclips in a TV current affairs segment (multimodal text). There may be one or more visual texts separate or attached to a print or online text that you will need to analyse. Visual texts can illustrate/complement/support/highlight points in a written text. For example, Figure 3.1 shows an example of a visual text accompanying the article, 'About Japanese whaling'.

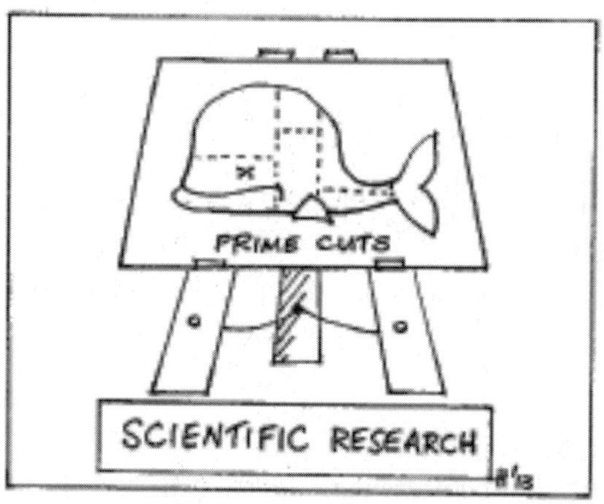

Figure 3.1

Points for visual analysis of whale cartoon in Figure 3.1:

- a cartoon that depicts a whale diagram like one used for meat in butcher's shops
- a 'prime cuts' body text supports butcher shop point
- a diagram on a stand like in a museum highlights treasured status
- a diagram mocks the 'scientific research' argument in a humorous way
- the cartoon contends that whales are being hunted for meat and not scientific research
- complements contention of accompanying article
- audience likely to laugh but then be concerned that the Japanese have no scientific reason for whaling; this may prompt them to sign a petition.

Visual language includes tone, the components of the visual, how they are framed, symbols, style and any verbal language like speech bubbles. It also includes any visual features related to the actual form of the text that help persuade and manipulate the reader. These features include watermarks, letterhead, logos, bullet points, mottos, bolding and italics. See the watermark of a dollar sign example in Figure 3.2.

> **MAKING MONEY WORK FOR YOU . . .**
>
> Now you've got some money, why not make your money work for you?
>
> Think of all the things that make you happy. Now, you can work towards achieving them. There are plenty of websites to give you good, sound, safe advice.
>
> Ever heard of compound interest? Sounds boring but, trust me, it could really work for you! All you need is $1 000 to get you going.
>
> The excitement of stocks and shares can be yours! Once you've invested your money you need not worry any more. Focus on enjoying the good things your money will buy while others do the worrying for you. But, you will need a plan.
>
> Start by writing down all the things you'll need money for. Mobile phone? iPod? Faster Internet connection? Overseas travel? A car? The deposit on an apartment?
>
> You do not need to give up everything to make all this a reality. You do need to understand, however, that future nancial happiness may involve a little present pain.
>
> Think of all the little things that we can really do without. What would it be for you? That 4 o'clock chocolate bar? That snappy new T-shirt? That 'must have' new hair product?
>
> It might cost a little bit now, but think about it: what price happiness?

Figure 3.2 Example of a watermark

When you analyse visual language and features, ask the following questions.

Visual language questions

1. What is the form of the visual? E.g. cartoon, photograph, graph.
2. What is the subject? What are they doing and saying?
3. How does visual complement, support, illustrate or contradict the contention in the accompanying written text?
4. What is the tone of the visual and how is this achieved? E.g. humorous?
5. What does body text and/or caption say?
6. What visual features, if any, are used in written text? E.g. bold, bullet points, water marks, italics
7. How does creator/author position the audience?
8. What is audience likely to think, feel or do when they look at visual?

Avoid writing the analysis of visuals in a separate paragraph. Weave visual language points throughout your language analysis; see Chapter 4.

Visual language terms explained

Visual language terms	Definition and how it persuades
Cartoon (form of visual)	Form of visual. Uses humour to add evidence, illustrate related aspect of issue or complement contention. Can present opposing viewpoint. May include caption, speech bubble or body text.
Composition	Number of items or subjects and their position within the text and in relation to one another. Includes camera angles, body language, white space, etc.
Framing	Literally how visual is framed, e.g. it is cropped to make subjects look crowded, bigger, smaller, close or far away. Can evoke emotional response from audience.
Focal point	Where audience's attention is drawn first. Can elicit sympathy or derision from audience for subject.
Colours and shading	Colours used, where, for whom? What do the colours symbolise?
Bold text	Highlights key words to the audience.
Bullet points	Emphasises main points to the audience.
Body text (verbal language)	Words within frame of text (e.g. speech bubbles, signs). Can reinforce or state contention.
Caption	Words outside the frame of the text. Can state contention.
Motifs, symbols, icons	Signature signs or labels that identify a subject. Images that represent ideas or concepts (e.g. a rose represents love, and a dove represents peace). An icon is a symbol or image of a sacred or religious subject. Dame Edna Everage is an Australian icon. Appeals to audience's sense of tradition and values.

Photograph	A form of visual language. Complements contention and/or argument in an accompanying text. Adds information and evidence or illustrates related aspects of the issue. May present emotional content. Framed carefully to position the audience to respond in certain way.
Italics	A visual feature. Often used to highlight a point. Can direct the reader's eye to a specific point.
Letterhead	A visual feature that outlines company or institute, usually at the top of a page. Can create the impression of status, authority and power that influences reader to agree with proposed action.
Logo	A visual feature that reflects a company or institute, often a part of letterhead. Can appeal to the reader's existing knowledge (e.g. the Nike tick and sense of 'cool') and make it easier for the audience to accept an idea or product. Presents the image of company or institute and is part of its branding. May appear modern or old-fashioned to an audience.
Stereotype	A type of generalisation in which a single person or thing is taken to represent a class of people or things. Generally well known to audience. The blonde, blue-eyed, suntanned, muscular lifesaver is said by some to be the stereotypical Australian. This is a generalisation and inaccurate. Not all Australians are blonde, blue-eyed, tanned, muscular lifesavers.
Symbols	Well-known symbols used in print texts, cartoons, etc., like captions, e.g. #, @ or #$@!!!
White space	How much blank space there is and where it's located. Where does it draw the audience's attention?
Watermark	Visual feature that is a mark or design in paper, visible beneath the written text, e.g. the word 'draft' written across some documents.
Style	The way the creator constructs the text (e.g. a minimal number of strokes and big round heads for a cartoon, or lots of close-up camera shots).
Layout	Different font sizes and percentage of text that is graphics. Can make message clearer to audience.

Practice activities

1 Analyse the following visual texts by answering the visual language questions (page 51).

2 Read the persuasive texts for the 2011 exam, 'The Power of Ink' in Chapter 4 and then answer the following guided questions to help you analyse how the persuasive strategies influence the audience.

The Power of Ink [VCAA 2011 exam]

A blog consists of a post and responses to the blog. Visuals can be included.

Guided analysis questions

1 List the four points of information given in the background information.
2 Who are 'followers' and how many does she have?
3 Why does Day use 'Ink' instead of tattoo in the headline?
4 Why is the title ironic?
5 What is contained in the byline and why is it bold?
6 Quote the inclusive/generalisation example in paragraph one.
7 How does Day connect with her audience?
8 How does Day make tattoos sound unattractive?
9 What type of shift does the line 'It was not always so' signal?
10 What historical evidence does Day offer?
11 Describe the form and subject of first visual.
12 What two important points does the caption of the first visual reveal?
13 What evidence is this visual linked to? How? Which response is it linked to?
14 What examples does Day give to show 'cruelty' of tattoos?
15 What does Day say causes us to 'develop a strong sense of satire'?
16 What historical example does she give of this satire?
17 How does she link historical example to a modern example?
18 What words does she use to say that tattoos have lost their individual value?

19 Why does Day include a reference to her own tattoo? What effect might this have on her readers?

20 What is Day's contention? How does it link to the headline?

21 What are two main points that Day uses to support her contention?

22 Which main point does the second visual support? How?

23 Who is Sam De Brito?

24 What words best describe Day's language style?

25 Which posted comment presents a clinical, authoritative argument that is likely to generate fear among readers? How does it do this?

26 How does Cleanskin support Day? Which other post does he support? How?

27 What point in Day's blog post does Kiwi's closing question reinforce? What are readers likely to feel and think when they read Kiwi's question?

28 Describe the tones used by Tash, Dr AB, Cleanskin and Kiwi. How do they sound?

29 Write two adjectives to describe the language used by each of Tash, Dr AB, Cleanskin and Kiwi?

30 What do you think that the readers might think about tattoos after reading the blog and responses? Why?

3 Select three current issues in the media and write an email for each issue using 'Your say' (at end of Chapter 2) as a guide. Include your contention and at least three different persuasive techniques for each email.

4 Create and complete the following language analysis overview for persuasive texts from one or more of the following language analysis tasks at the end of Chapter 4.

- *A Word from our Coach ...* [VCAA 2008 English exam]
- Digital Technology >Voxi >>*Keyed In* [VCAA 2009 English exam]
- *Chickens Range Free* [VCAA 2008 sample English exam, modified]
- *Mobiles Immobilised* [VCAA 2004 English exam, modified]
- *Are We Overprotected?* [VCAA 2007 English exam]
- *FINished with Fins*
- *The Power of Ink* [VCAA 2011 English exam]
- *Reading: The Future* [VCAA 2012 English exam] Chapter 9
- *Getting our future back on the rails – slowly* [VCAA 2013 English exam] Chapter 11

Language analysis overview chart

<table>
<tr><td colspan="3">Issue:
Contention

Outline
Audience
Style – form and language
Tone(s)</td></tr>
<tr><td>Arguments/main points</td><td>Persuasive strategies (techniques & appeals)</td><td>Likely audience impact (what they might think, feel, believe, do)</td></tr>
<tr><td>1</td><td></td><td></td></tr>
<tr><td>2</td><td></td><td></td></tr>
<tr><td>3</td><td></td><td></td></tr>
<tr><td>Additional if needed</td><td></td><td></td></tr>
<tr><td>Conclusion</td><td></td><td></td></tr>
</table>

Chapter 4

How to write a language analysis

Instructions for Section C

Section C requires students to analyse the ways in which language and visual features are used to present a point of view.

Read the following material and then complete the task below.

Write your analysis as a coherently structured piece of prose.

Your response will be assessed according to the criteria set out in this book.

Section C is worth one-third of the total assessment for the examination.

TASK

How is written and visual language used to attempt to persuade the audience to share the point of view of the speaker? [VCAA English 2012 exam]

- There may be three or more persuasive texts.
- There may be different points of view.
- A persuasive text may be a photograph, letter, editorial, blog, and so on.
- There will always be at least one visual text for you to analyse.

EAL TASK

Part 1

Write a note-form summary of the speech by Mrs Elliot. Your response must be in note form. Do not use complete sentences.

Part 2

Write a piece of prose that explains how language and visual features have been used in the speech by Mrs Elliot to attempt to persuade the audience about three of the main points in the speech. [VCAA English 2012 exam]

High-scoring language analysis requirements

- demonstrate an understanding of issue and context (the big picture)
- show *what* points of view, contention and arguments are presented
- show *how* written and visual language is used to persuade audience
- show *what* audience is likely to believe, think, feel and do
- use a clear and logical structure with precise metalanguage.

Six steps to language analysis

1	Examine the background information.
2	Mark up persuasive texts and identify: • *what* is the writer's POV, contention and argument • *how* the writer uses persuasive language and techniques.
3	Stereotype (in your head) the target audience and determine the likely impact.
4	Decide the analysis structure, i.e. basic (mini weave), semi weave or total weave structure.
5	Write 800–1200 words.
6	Review and edit.

1 Examine background information

Read the background information carefully and find answers to the following:

- What is the issue?
- What event sparked the issue?
- Why were texts created?
- Who is the target audience?
- What is the author's role and expertise regarding issue?

2 Mark up texts

Read persuasive texts more than once and mark up (identify) using your own code the:

- (different) points of view
- contentions
- arguments
- persuasive language and techniques
- visual language and features
- conventions of form structure
- tone and tonal shift.

Suggested analysis mark-up code

- Underline or bracket contention and write (C).
- Number arguments, e.g. (Arg 1), (Arg 2).
- Highlight or write (F) for facts and number them.
- Identify techniques, e.g. (R) for repetition, (G) for generalisation, (Ap) for appeals, (EL) for emotive language, (INC) for inclusive language.

- Add comments in margins about *how* it persuades and its likely impact on the audience.
- Label visuals using correct visual terms, e.g. foreground, body text or caption, and link them to written points and contention.
- Circle words that indicate tone. Identify tonal shifts, e.g. a rhetorical question may signal a change in tone.
- Identify visual features of form (e.g. greeting, call to action, byline, headline, bullet points, logo or watermark) and link to the tone and contention.

Background information

Helen Day is a part-time journalist and blogger. She maintains her blog entitled *Street Beat* in which she comments on a variety of current social issues. This blog entry, *The Power of Ink*, is about tattoos and it has drawn a variety of responses from readers of her blog.

The Power of Ink

FRIDAY 25 MARCH 2011

Once a sign of deviance and criminality, they're now a fashion statement.

Everyone has tattoos these days: even me. I live near a mega shopping centre and every time I visit, I see enough ink on suburban housewives to outdo the collection in any Australian prison.

FOLLOWERS

There are 12,615 followers

Figure 4.1 Marked-up sample

3 Stereotype audience and determine likely impact

1 Stereotype the target audience in your head. What is their gender? Age? General likes and dislikes? Cultural and social values?

2 Imagine you are the target audience.
   - *How* does the text makes you feel and think about issue?
   - *How* does the text appeal to your emotions? E.g. does it appeal to your parental sense of responsibility for their children? Does it appeal to your frustration about the government?
   - Does it appeal to your compassion about your fellow human beings?
   - Does it appeal to your sense of justice? Fairness?
   - *What* might you do as a result of being persuaded by the writer? E.g.
     – Are you likely to feel guilt or fear?
     – Are you likely to follow an expert's advice?
     – Are you likely to protest to the government or council?

(See Chapter 3 for a list of appeals and more information.)

4 Decide the analysis structure

The way you structure your analysis depends on your writing skills and the number and length of the written texts you have to analyse. See Chapter 2 for diagrams of eight possible persuasive text forms (Figures 2.1 to 2.8) and a table of persuasive forms used in exams from 2008 to 2013.

If you have more than one written text to analyse, the general rule of thumb is that you allot the same percentage of words to your analysis as the percentage of words used in the persuasive text.

Example 1

Persuasive text: Article (750 words) with a photograph plus email response (250 words)

Your analysis would spend about 75% of the total time analysing the article and photograph, and 25% on the email response.

Example 2

Persuasive text: Blog post with two visuals (700 words) plus four responses (200 words)

Your analysis would comprise about 75% of the total analysing the article and two visuals and 25% on the four responses. The blog post and visuals would be Text 1 and the four responses would be together as Text 2.

Different teachers have different language analysis styles that they like students to use. For example, some teachers encourage students to structure body paragraphs with their topic sentences about arguments and main points, while other teachers prefer their students to structure the paragraphs around appeals.

There are three general structures for language analysis that you can use and they can easily incorporate your teacher's preferred language analysis style. Template versions of these three structures are in Chapter 4.

1 Basic language analysis (Mini weave)

- Include COAST (contention, outline, audience, style & tone) in your introduction.
- Include references to all written and visual texts in your introduction.
- Weave visual language analysis to support points throughout your analysis.

- Use link words and structure verbs to ensure that analysis reads logically.
- This is the easiest weave to do.

Suits: Long written text plus visuals, e.g. speech plus slides or one article plus visuals

2 Semi weave structure

- Include COAST (see above) for *all* written texts and refer to visuals in your introduction.
- Analyse each written text separately in its own body paragraphs.
- Use visual language analysis woven throughout to support points.
- Use link words and structure verbs to ensure that analysis reads logically.
- The conclusion should give a general comparison between the texts including: restated contentions and overall impact.

Note: Sometimes you may need two or three body paragraphs to analyse one long text.

Suits: One longer written text and visuals plus a smaller text, e.g. blog with visuals and one or several smaller posts. Also suits two or three texts of similar length e.g. article, letter and visual.

Note: If there are several smaller texts like three responses to an article or blog, then they can be grouped together as one text.

3 Total weave structure

- Includes COAST (see above) for *all* written texts and refer to visuals in your introduction.
- Body paragraphs weave comparisons from all texts.
- Use link words and structure verbs to ensure that analysis reads logically.
- Use visual language analysis woven throughout to support points.
- The conclusion should give a general comparison between the texts including: restated contentions and overall impact.
- This is the most difficult analysis to write.

Suits: Two or three texts of similar length, e.g. article and letter and advertisement, or one long written text and several smaller texts.

Note: The introductions for the semi weave and total weave are the same.

Try to avoid writing using a block structure (analysing each written and visual text in separate paragraphs) as it lacks cohesion and looks like separate mini analyses.

5 Write

Aim for five to seven paragraphs (800–1200 words). Remember that you need to use formal language (don't write how you speak) as well as precise metalanguage and that you cannot analyse every single technique.

Follow 'Top 10 language analysis hints' and 'Useful analysis language' where you will find examples of language analysis structure, contention, audience and 'how' verbs as well as sentence starters. If handwriting, consider leaving two lines at the start and between paragraphs, and not writing on the last line. This makes it easier to read your work and allows you to include any points you may have missed.

Top 10 language analysis hints

1 Select persuasive strategies that most influence the arguments.
2 Include COAST in intro: **C**ontention, **O**utline, **A**udience, **S**tyle, **T**one.
3 Describe overall tone and any tonal shifts.
4 Write topic sentences that include subject matter, tone and structure verbs.
5 Ensure that body paragraphs address *what* is said and *how* it is likely to impact on audience.
6 Use present tense and appropriate metalanguage (key terms).
7 Link your analysis of visual language and features to written points and weave throughout analysis.
8 Think 'quote fest'. Weave small quotes throughout. Avoid big chunks.
9 Use link words and connectives so that your analysis is cohesive and doesn't look like a Frankenstein's monster essay – several separate paragraphs badly stitched together.
10 Use the writer's full name the first time, e.g. Ellen McQueen, then the surname thereafter.

What *not* to do!

- Do not try to analyse everything and do not include your opinion.
- Avoid writing all the visual language analysis in the one paragraph.
- Avoid just labelling (listing) persuasive techniques and language.
- Avoid copying sentence-long quotes, and don't repeat quotes.
- Avoid just writing a summary of the text(s) using quotes. You need to discuss 'how' the words you've quoted impact on audience.
- Do not start every sentence with 'the writer'. Use their name.

6 Review and edit

Check your analysis for grammar, spelling and punctuation errors. Make sure that it is structured logically. Use the following DIY rubric for language analysis, language analysis checklist and PETs at the end of this chapter to help you.

DIY language analysis general rubric

High level response	Mid-level response	Low-level response
Demonstrates understanding of background information, e.g. form, author, audience, event.	Some understanding of context (background information).	Little or no understanding of context (background information).
Identifies contention and comments on arguments/main points.	Identifies contention. Little or no comment on arguments/main points.	Little or no understanding of contention.
Analyses *how* language persuades and likely impact on audience and *how* audience is positioned.	Analyses *how* language persuades. Limited analysis of likely impact on audience.	Labels persuasive techniques. No discussion of likely audience impact.
Comments on structure of text, e.g. opens, concludes, continues.	Include some comments on structure of text.	Includes no reference to structure of text at all.
Weaves visual language and features throughout analysis to support or contradict arguments.	Includes reference to visual language in separate paragraph only.	Includes no reference to visual language at all.
Weaves small quotes in sentences to support points throughout analysis.	Includes some quotes to support points throughout analysis.	No quotes included to support analysis.
Analyses tone and tonal shift(s).	Analyses tone but makes no reference to tonal shift(s).	Does not mention tone and/or tonal shift(s).

Basic language analysis (Mini weave structure)

Introduction (doesn't need to be in this order) **C**ontention **O**utline of issue (event or trigger. 1–2 lines) **A**udience **S**tyle: sentence that includes visual text and written text (form) and overall language style (2 or 3 most effective persuasive techniques) **T** one – overall (mention tonal shift if necessary)
Body para 1 Topic sentence: structure verb + main point (argument) + tone **What** (Quote) writer says (Techniques and/or appeals) **How** it positions audience **What** is likely audience impact? (likely to believe, feel or do?) Weave in visual language, if relevant.
Body para 2 Topic sentence: structure verb + main point (argument) + tone + tone **What** (Quote) writer says (Techniques and/or appeals) **How** it positions audience **What** is likely audience impact? (likely to believe, feel or do?) Weave in visual language, if relevant.
Body para 3 Topic sentence: structure verb + main point (argument) + tone **What** (Quote) writer says (Techniques and/or appeals) **How** it positions audience **What** is the likely audience impact? (likely to believe, feel or do?) Weave in visual language, if relevant.
Conclusion (smaller than intro) • Link word/Connective • Restate contention • Overall language style • Overall likely impact on the audience

Semi weave structure

Introduction
Weave COAST for all texts, e.g. Texts 1, 2 and 3
Contention
Outline of issue
Audience
Style: weave visual text and written text (form) and language style
Tone: overall
Note: Only write outline and target audience once.

Body paragraph 1
Text 1 analysis
Topic sentence: structure verb + argument/main point or appeal + tone
What (Quote) writer says (techniques)
How it positions audience
What is likely audience impact?
Weave visual language to support written points.

Connective
Body paragraph 2
Text 1 analysis cont. or Text 2
Topic sentence: structure verb + argument/main point or appeal + tone
What (quote) writer says
How it positions audience
What is likely audience impact?
Weave visual language to support written points.

Connective
Body paragraph 3
Text 2 analysis/Text 3 analysis
Topic sentence: structure verb + argument/main point or appeal + tone
What (quote) writer says (techniques)
How it positions audience
What is likely audience impact?
Weave visual language to support written points.

Total weave structure

Introduction
Weave COAST for all texts, e.g. Texts 1, 2 and 3
Contention
Outline of issue
Audience
Style: weave visual text and written text (form) and language style
Tone: overall
Note: Only write outline and target audience once.

Body paragraphs X 3 or 4
Each body para should contain the following:
Topic sentence = Text 1 structure verb + argument/main point or appeal + tone
What (quote) writer says (techniques)
How it positions audience
What is likely audience impact

Connective (compare/contrast)
Text 2 structure verb + argument/main point or appeal + tone.
What (quote) writer says (techniques)
How it positions audience
What is likely audience impact

Connective (compare/contrast)
Text 3 structure verb + argument/main point or appeal + tone.
What (quote) writer says (techniques)
How it positions audience
What is likely audience impact

- **Connectives** to be used throughout
- Weave visual language to support written points

Conclusion
Compare/contrast Texts 1 and 2.
- Contentions
- Overall language style
- Likely impact on the audience

Conclusion
Compare/contrast Texts 1 and 2.
- Contentions
- Overall language style
- Likely impact on the audience

Introductions

Your introduction is the most important part of your analysis as it sets up your piece. A well-written introduction creates a favourable impression with examiners.

Hints
- Include COAST (or whatever acronym your teacher uses)
- When comparing texts, avoid writing 'contends' twice. Use different contention verbs.
- Always include a reference to visual(s).
- Include tonal shifts if you can, e.g. 'combines a tone that shifts from friendly to ominous with …'
- Always use formal language and correct metalanguage.
- Reread your introduction carefully and neatly edit any mistakes.
- If you need to make massive changes, rewrite your introduction.

General template
If you are not sure how to write your introduction use the following template as a starting point until you become confident and write your own style.

Recently the issue of [NAME ISSUE] has been addressed in the media. In her [FORM] in [NAME OF PUBLICATION/OCCASION], [AUTHOR] contends that [CONTENTION PARTIALLY QUOTED IF POSSIBLE]. [AUTHOR] combines a [TONE WORD] tone with [MAIN PERSUASIVE TECHNIQUE 1], [MAIN PERSUASIVE TECHNIQUE 2] and an accompanying visual (s) in an attempt to convince her [AUDIENCE] that [OVERALL COMMENT ABOUT ISSUE].

Teenage gambling – sample using template

Recently the issue of teenage gambling was addressed in the community with the distribution of a brochure from the Victorian Responsible Gambling Foundation. In her presentation to Moortown Secondary College's Parents Group, former principal Rose Larkin contends that because the internet and smart phones mean that 'there are more ways to gamble now', it is up to the parents to demonstrate 'responsible behaviour and values' to their children. Larkin combines an authoritative tone with alarming facts, personal examples and accompanying visuals in an attempt to convince parents about the serious nature of the issue and the importance of their role.

NAME ISSUE
AUTHOR
FORM
CONTENTION PARTIALLY QUOTED
TONE
MAIN PERSUASIVE TECHNIQUES
OVERALL COMMENT ABOUT ISSUE

Figure 4.2
(ANNOTATED – Teenage sample using template)

Mini weave introduction

A word from our coach ... [VCAA 2008 exam]

The issue of good sportsmanship allows a coach from a local sports club to address the larger issue of 'good' parent versus 'bad' parent and the effect on children and the club, in the new season's first newsletter, after poor sportsmanship in the previous season has discouraged volunteers. Coach Sam contends in his column that 'the only goal that should matter in kids' sport is the promotion of good sportsmanship' and that parents have a responsibility to role model good behaviour, 'before, during and after the game'. Coach Sam uses his experience and position together with a confident tone, informal style and accompanying cartoon to explain the importance of good sportsmanship to his target audience of parents.

- *Mini weave analysis*
- *Includes reference to written and visual texts in introduction*
- *Persuasive texts: newsletter with cartoon*

Semi and total weave introduction

The Power of Ink [VCAA 2011 exam]

Helen Day's popular blog, Street Beat, has used social media to discuss the changing attitudes towards tattoos. In her post, 'The Power of Ink', Day contends in an authoritative and confident tone that the tattoo has lost its connotations of 'deviance' and 'criminality' as they have become 'a fashion statement'. Day appeals to her 12 615 strong readership and targets younger readers in particular through her language choices and accompanying visuals aimed at causing her blog followers to think before getting tattoos for trivial reasons. The four comments in response to Day's post use a range of tones from upbeat to hurtful and variously claim that tattoos are 'unique', not 'individual', culturally significant and have associated medical risks. Three of the comments clearly support Day's point of view as an older person while Tash's comment exemplifies Day's earlier thinking about tattoos.

- *Could be a sample from a semi weave or total weave analysis.*
- *The above introduction weaves COAST for all written and visual texts.*
- *Includes reference to visual language.*
- *Refers to visual feature '12 615' readers.*
- *Persuasive texts = one blog post which contains two visuals, visual features and four comments. For the purpose of analysis, the four comments have been put together as one text.*

Body paragraphs

You may have 3–5 body paragraphs and may be of varying length. Your body paragraphs generally begin with topic sentences that feature the following:

1 Structure verb or connective + argument + tone

2 Structure verb or connective + appeal + tone

Whichever way you start your body paragraph you need to include:

- *What* is said (quotes and techniques)
- *How* it positions audience
- *What* is likely impact on audience

Use **SATER** to help you

S tructure verb

A rgument (main point)/Appeal

T echnique(s) – don't label every technique

E vidence [quotes]

R elate to audience position and impact

Hints

- Clearly structure your topic sentences
- Do not include every technique
- Do not quote giant slabs but weave smaller quotes in where relevant
- Paraphrasing sometimes is OK
- Do not merely write a summary of text that includes brief quotes.
- Weave in visual analysis.
- Comment on how audience is positioned and the likely impact but not for every technique. Think bigger picture.

Body template

[WRITER'S NAME] begins/opens her [FORM] by [ADVERB] stating that [MAIN POINT 1/ARGUMENT 1] which signals to/connects with her [AUDIENCE]. She appeals to their sense of [APPEAL] using [QUOTE AND/OR PERSUASIVE TECHNIQUE]. The cartoon in which [CREATOR'S NAME] depicts [BRIEF DESCRIPTION OF CARTOON] supports this point as [GIVE REASON WHY]. [POINT FROM VISUAL] is likely to evoke feelings of [DESCRIBE EMOTION LINKED TO APPEAL] which may encourage [AUDIENCE] to [LIKELY ACTION, BELIEF OF AUDIENCE].

Conclusions

While not as important as your introduction, you nevertheless need a conclusion to your analysis. Your conclusion should include:

- Restated contention(s) – using different words
- Most effective persuasive devices and/or language style

- How audience is positioned
- Overall likely impact = emotion or appeal of text(s)
- Mention big picture possible implications

If you are analysing one extended text with two accompanying visuals then you can begin your conclusion with the text's final point e.g. 'Dr Maxwell concludes his presentation by challenging his fellow scientists to [QUOTE – CALL TO ACTION.' Then continue by adding the above points.

Weave Conclusion Style 1 Template

While [TEXT ONE AUTHOR'S NAME] [FORM] asserts that [CONTENTION] using [MOST EFFECTIVE PERSUASIVE DEVICES] and [VISUAL], [TEXT TWO AUTHOR'S NAME] responds with /challenges this with [CONTENTION] and consistently / repeatedly employs a [MOST EFFECTIVE PERSUASIVE DEVICES]. [TEXT ONE AUTHOR'S NAME] [FORM] positions audience to feel [EMOTIONAL APPEAL] and may [AUDIENCE IMPACT] whereas [TEXT TWO AUTHOR'S NAME] [FORM] is likely to [AUDIENCE POSITION & IMPACT] when [INCLUDE BIG PICTURE IMPLICATIONS]

Weave Conclusion Style 2 Template

[TEXT ONE AUTHOR'S NAME] [FORM] with its accompanying [VISUAL] and [TEXT TWO AUTHOR'S NAME] [FORM] discuss the [ADJECTIVE] issue of [ISSUE]. [TEXT ONE AUTHOR'S NAME] [FORM] [ADVERB] employs [MOST EFFECTIVE PERSUASIVE DEVICES] and [VISUAL] which positions audience to [EMOTIONAL APPEAL] and may [AUDIENCE IMPACT]. [CONNECTIVE e.g. In contrast, Unlike, On the other hand] [TEXT TWO AUTHOR'S NAME] [FORM] [**REFERENCE text one somehow**] which [POSITION VERB] likely [AUDIENCE IMPACT]. [BIG PICTURE IMPLICATIONS]

Sample conclusion – one extended text

The leader of the Grow Slow Garden Group concludes his newsletter by 'urging' the Council to take the 'visionary step of voting for the garden'. In a positive and enthusiastic tone he requests that the community 'join in' and make the garden a 'success'. His final inclusive statement is likely to convince householders that this is a 'rare' chance for them to 'get together and work towards a common goal', influencing them to take the 'opportunity' to be instrumental in creating a 'healthier future, for ourselves, our children and our planet.'

Sample conclusion – several texts

Day's blog post and readers' comments discuss the issue of the significance and power of tattoos. Day concludes her argument by restating her realisation that while tattoos are now commonplace, some tattoos are special and have 'cultural significance'. Her use of facts, both historical and modern combined with personal anecdote evokes strong responses from her readers. These various responses from her followers reinforce aspects of her argument and are likely to encourage her followers to think twice about getting a tattoo.

Figure 4.3
SAMPLE CONCLUSION – ONE EXTENDED TEXT (ANNOTATED)
SAMPLE CONCLUSION – SEVERAL TEXTS (ANNOTATED)

Language analysis cheat sheet

INTRODUCTION Contention Outline: context - issue? Event? When? Audience Style: form + language and/or 2 techniques most used+ visuals Tone: overall **Use present tense**	**Outline:** 'Recently the [issue] …' 'In reference to the recent discussion/legislation/concern [issue]…' **Contention verbs**: contends, asserts, claims, states e.g. 'In her letter to the editor, Janice King contends that …' 'Voxi claims, in her online piece, …' **Form:** speech, blog, article, accompanying visual(s) **Tone**: friendly, authoritative, concerned, humorous **Language:** personal, formal, emotive, informal **Style, tone and audience** e.g.'Voxi combines a confident tone with inclusive language, popular examples and accompanying visual to engage her online readers who are "net savvy".'
BODY 3–5 paragraphs Each paragraph starts: structure verb + argument/appeal + tone *What* is said (quote and techniques) *How* it positions audience *What* is likely impact on audience? **Weave *visual* analysis into body paragraphs, and *not* in one separate para.**	**Start structure:** King opens/begins his blog … 'The headline, "Chickens range free" is a pun …' ***How* verbs:** demonstrates, signals, uses, provides 'Coach Sam uses strong language to describe some parents as "toxic parents" who "poison" the club.' **Middle structure words:** continues, further argues 'In response to Carter's article, Dr Zingh states … ' **Link words/connectives:** In contrast, unlike, conversely, furthermore, as well as, similarly. 'In contrast, May Brown's subtle rational approach is strengthened by her appeals to family values.' **Visual verbs**: depicts, highlights, supports 'The cropped photograph of three chickens cramped into a tiny cage clearly demonstrates the "inhumane" conditions described by Smith.' **Audience impact**: positions the reader to, appeals to the reader's sense of [appeal], encourages, compels 'The photo of a homeless man "sleeping rough" appeals to the reader's sense of compassion and may encourage them to donate to the charity.'
CONCLUSION Analyse writer's final point. Restate contention (in different words) Overall likely audience impact.	**Conclusion** words: finishes, concludes, closes. 'Dr Maxwell concludes his speech about new technology by inviting his audience to …' 'By appealing to his audience's sense of excitement and using a consistent upbeat tone Dr Maxwell is able to draw readers onside to view the new technology as beneficial and to cast doubt on those who experience anxiety at the sudden changes.'

Useful analysis language

Outline sentences

An outline sentence starts your analysis. It addresses the 'big picture' and may introduce the event or incident that sparked the issue as well as the author and form. Make sure that your outline sentence is linked to your contention. You can do this by repeating the form and/or using a pronoun instead of repeating the author's name.

Outline example linked to contention

Helen Day's popular blog, *Street Beat,* uses social media to discuss the changing attitudes towards tattoos. In her recent entry Day contends to her followers that …

Outline examples

- Recently the issue of [NAME OF ISSUE]
- The closure of a railway line in a local community has generated discussion among locals as to the future uses of the land the line occupied.
- In reference to the recent discussion about [ISSUE]
- The issue of good sportsmanship allows Coach Sam to address the larger issue of 'good' parent versus 'bad' parent and the effect on children and the club in the new season's first newsletter.
- The 2002 commitment to achieve a 'significant reduction in the rate of biodiversity loss' by 2010 has prompted a review of the progress achieved in order to 'take stock' and promote a sustainable future.

Verbs identifying contention

contends states suggests challenges asserts claims
advocates attempts to …

Contention examples

- In her letter to the editor, Deb Farrelly strongly contends that …
- Professor Lee, in his keynote speech at the International Biodiversity Conference, asserts that …
- In an online opinion piece, Voxi claims that the impact of digital technology is a positive one.
- Part-time blogger TJ states, in his popular blog, that …
- [Author A] contends that … while [author B] rejects the view that …
- [Author A] contends that … while [author B] claims that …

NB: Use a partial quote when writing the contention or paraphrase contention.

Tone advice

It is essential that you analyse tone and any tonal shifts. You need to refer to tone more than once in your analysis. While you should refer to tone and/or tonal shift in your introduction, you also need to refer to tone throughout your analysis and comment on *how* it helps position the audience and *how* and *when* it changes or shifts. Ask yourself, 'How does the writer sound?' Avoid using the words, 'neutral', 'positive' or 'negative' to describe tone if you can and use more specific words instead. Use the following tone chart to help you.

Tone chart

Questions about tone	**Tone words**
Is writer trying to connect with audience?	Friendly, amicable, benevolent, sympathetic, empathetic, engaging, sincere, familiar, warm
Does writer sound positive?	Upbeat, optimistic, approving, cheerful, appreciative, frank, forthright, respectful, earnest
Is writer trying to scare or warn audience?	Concerned, determined, shocked, alarmed, ominous (warning)
Is writer an expert?	Authoritative, confident, strident, matter-of-fact
Is writer trying to be funny?	Humorous, wry, satirical, ironical, sarcastic, sardonic
Is writer committed to a cause?	Passionate, earnest, enthusiastic, zealous, fervent, spirited
Is writer against governments and big institutions?	Frustrated, cynical, confrontational
Does writer sound angry?	Aggressive, outraged, hostile, scathing, vindictive, vitriolic, forceful, critical, forceful, abusive, disgusted
Does writer sound like they miss a time when they thought the world was a better place?	Nostalgic, sentimental, wistful, whimsical
Does writer sound smug? Conceited?	Patronising, condescending, arrogant, self-righteous, moralising, preaching, heavy-handed, mocking
Does writer sound neutral?	Measured, controlled, calm, detached, reasoned, moderate, diplomatic, cautious, rational

Does writer sound sad?	Sombre, regretful, disappointed, distressed, nostalgic
Does writer sound uncertain?	Puzzled, confused, questioning, bewildered
Does writer sound respectful?	Open-minded, sympathetic, supportive, patriotic, apologetic, understanding, empathetic, sincere
Does writer sound like they think Australia is the best place on Earth?	Jingoistic, patriotic

Tone examples

- In contrast to the [author X's] letter, [author Y's] personal column adopts a reasoned, almost regretful tone.
- [Author X] seeks, with an enthusiastic tone, …
- Unlike [author X], [author Y] utilises a more informal, emotive tone to …
- Unlike Carter's didactic tone, Ambrose employs a confident yet friendly tone to engage his readers
- There is a tonal shift in the mid section of the speech after Lee establishes the purpose for the conference, where his tone shifts from concerned to increasingly alarmed ...
- Voxi combines a conversational tone with personal language to engage her audience of online readers who are 'net savvy'.
- Smith employs a tonal shift from friendly to authoritative when referring to statistics about the number of hours teenagers spend gaming …
- Using a rational yet fearful tone in places, Dr Catalano explains …
- There is a tonal shift as Day generates a historical context for her contemporary audience.
- The irreverent cartoon complements the humorous tone and the contention of the article.
- The rhetorical question, 'so what's to worry about?' signals a tonal shift from upbeat to concerned.
- The friendly tone of the column is established from the start with [example].

Language style

Language style is the overall style of the text(s), the author's individual voice. It may include form and its conventions and visual language. Some students who have difficulty describing the overall language style concentrate instead on describing the three predominant persuasive techniques combined with tone and visual language. Other students describe the form, visual language and overall approach. Some students describe form and overall tone.

Forms

Written: letter to the editor, article, blog, posts, email, editorial, online opinion piece, transcript of speech, personal column, newsletter (see Chapter 2).

Visual: photograph, cartoon, sketch, graph, sign, table (see Chapter 3).
Some visual features are the watermark, logo, letterhead, bullet point and bold typeface.

It's important to refer to the visual language in your introduction, as part of the weaving process. See the following language style examples, and see Chapter 2 for more Language style advice.

Words to describe language style

assertive	evocative	simplistic	ambiguous	difficult	ironic
exaggerated	colourful	graphic	stereotypical	cynical	emotive
precise	logical	convoluted	formal	informal	personal

Language style examples

- Written in first person, McQueen combines facts with a humorous tone and visual language that offers both insight into and an explanation for the Japanese way of thinking about whaling.

- Mrs Elliot uses her expertise as a retired librarian–teacher together with a direct and personal approach to persuade her audience that …

- Voxi combines a conversational and confident tone with inclusive language, popular examples and accompanying photographs to appeal to her audience of online readers who are 'net savvy'.

- Day appeals to her 12 615-strong readership and targets her younger 'followers' in particular though appealing visuals, language choices and cautious stance, and aims to convince her blog followers to think before obtaining tattoos for trivial reasons.

- Newton combines a friendly, then authoritative tone with several slides, numerous facts and logical language in an attempt to convince his audience of parents about the dangers of videogaming.

Topic sentence examples

- Lee invites his audience's consternation and involvement in the issue by asking them to reflect on whether this has been achieved through the use of repetition, 'has this?' followed by the revealing question, 'honestly, how well have we done?' (emotion + subject + persuasive technique)

- There is a tonal shift in the mid section of the speech as Lee's tone shifts from concerned to alarmed when he presents disturbing statistics of [example]. (tone + persuasive technique/argument)

- Lee deliberately makes delegates uncomfortable by describing their current approach as 'haphazard', which has strong associations with mistakes and poor planning. (emotion + persuasive language + argument)

- There is a tonal shift as Day generates a historical context for her contemporary audience. (tone + subject matter)

- Mrs Elliot closes her speech with an extended personal anecdote of her experience reading Harry Potter on a long haul flight to London, allowing her to further her description of reading possessing magical properties as 'time itself began to fly'. (structure verb + persuasive language + subject matter description)

- Using a familiar and warm tone, Bale is able to entice the readers with his anecdotes which promote the health and safety of children. (tone + persuasive language + position audience)

'How' verbs

Verbs that discuss *how* a particular example of written or visual language is used include:

demonstrates	indicates	reflects	suggests	provides
highlights	signals	describes	exemplifies	suggests
represents	shows	signposts	mirrors	uses/employs

'How' verbs examples

- Mrs Elliot mirrors her imagery of children going to school minus the physical burden of 'their great big textbooks' with a photograph of a school-aged child connected to an e-book and leaning against a stack of thick books.
- The simile 'as empty and unwholesome as a packet of potato chips' links Mrs Elliot's concern for 'kids' with obesity, another high-profile concern of Australia's youth.

- Voxi negatively describes 'some people' to her readers as 'suspicious', 'afraid, 'predictable' and 'older people', then finally as 'losers'.
- Coach Sam uses strong language and divides parents into two categories; 'toxic parents' who suffer from 'sports rage' and are 'poisoning our club', and the 'good parents' who model and encourage good sportsmanship.
- The use of the word 'crisis' has negative connotations of disaster and chaos, evoking feelings of unease within readers who may face problems if …

Visual language examples

- The photograph of three chickens cramped into a tiny cage clearly demonstrates the 'inhumane conditions' described by Smith.
- Cartoonist Connolly depicts the AFL coach as wearing a giant rhinoceros' skin as part of his role in his cartoon employing a humorous tone to …
- Such a confronting image of [BRIEF DESCRIPTION], like Coach Sam firmly states, shows that …
- The image of [BRIEF DESCRIPTION] represents [the author's] desire for a more compassionate society where …
- The words '[example]' in the speech bubble in the cartoon reinforce …
- The caption '[example]' supports [AUTHOR'S NAME] …
- The 'blanket' in the photograph is a visual representation of the 'Blanket of indifference' in the headline.
- The graphic image of [example] complements the contention/point that …
- Like [writer], photographer/cartoonist highlights …

Adverbs

Adverbs add more meaning to verbs. Include some adverbs in your analysis so that your vocabulary sounds more sophisticated.

Examples

Dr Jiang contends — Dr Jiang *strongly* contends
Mr Southgate protests — Mr Southgate *repeatedly* protests
Senator Keats provides a list of complaints that include [QUOTE]
Senator Keats *disapprovingly* provides a list of complaints that include [QUOTE]
Maloney asserts that [CONTENTION]
Maloney *rationally* asserts that [CONTENTION]
Physiotherapist Laumets argues that performance enhancing drugs [QUOTE]
Physiotherapist Laumets l*ogically* argues that performance enhancing drugs [QUOTE]
Professional surfer Watson, asks the question [QUOTE] …
Professional surfer Watson, *deliberately* asks the question [QUOTE] …

Tennis star, Mat Duchini, stated [QUOTE]
Tennis star, Mat Duchini, *emphatically* stated [QUOTE]

Connectives

Connectives are connecting words that help you link points in your analysis.

Connectives chart

Adds similar points	**Emphasises points**	**Compares points**
And In addition Also Moreover As well as	In particular Especially Above all Notably	In the same way Similarly Like In comparison to
Contrasts points	**Sequences points (signposts)**	**Summarises points**
Instead of On the other hand Conversely Nevertheless But	First Second Last, finally Introducing Initially After Next	In summary In short In brief
Explains why	**Illustrates points**	**Qualifies points**
Because So consequently As a result	For example For instance For this reason in case of Just as	Although However Unless Yet Apart from

Linked points examples

- In addition to questioning the lack of compassion by the population towards battery caged chickens, Smith employs expert Jeremy Bentham to question, ‘Can they suffer?’
- In contrast, May Brown’s subtle rational approach is strengthened by her appeals to family and educational values.
- Furthermore, by tying his concern to ‘human wellbeing’ the delegates’ fears are further heightened as the ‘extinction’ is now also connected with humans.

Audience impact verbs

influences generates creates encourages compels positions manipulates appeals evokes provokes polarise alienate elicits incites

Audience impact examples

- … is likely to evoke sympathy/compassion in his audience of parents by appealing to their sense of parental responsibility.
- By introducing the controversial example of 'acceptable verbal abuse' Inspector Daniel positions his audience to question their own behaviour.
- Dr Catalano's repeated references to the WADA findings influences his readers to accept the view that some cyclists continued to 'dope' after 2010.
- Slides of recent statistics detailing alarming increase in child obesity is likely to shock parents and result in them seeking further guidance about nutrition.
- Morgan's photograph of a homeless man 'sleeping rough' appeals to the reader's sense of compassion and may encourage them to donate to the charity.
- Scientist Ed Jin's use of repeated rhetorical question 'Can we do more?' attempts to make the audience feel uncomfortable about their obvious lack of effort concerning the environment and manipulate them into adopting one of the two courses of recommended action.
- Using repeated rhetorical questions, [quote] Mitch Hoar compels his followers to share his sense of outrage at the new petrol tax.
- While some members of the audience may be excited at the prospect of new technology, others may experience anxiety at changes happening too fast.
- Professor Mason uses a gruesome photograph of a de-finned and dead shark at the start of her article to shock the beachside community.
- Principal Wheeler flatters supporters of banning mobile phones in classes by referring to them as 'more academically orientated', which positions those parents who disagree with his ban as …
- Although some readers would easily understand the technical jargon, others may not and would probably feel excluded from the debate.
- Mr Oswald's warm salutation, 'Good morning, fellow book-lovers', quickly imbues his target audience with a sense of community, and, as such, invites them to share his concern.
- Clayton's anecdote personalises the issue, enabling him to connect to his audience, having shared the same experience.
- Dr Catalano appeals to his audience's sense of logic by presenting the recent facts and statistics on the use of EPO by athletes, which is likely to result in their scepticism about winning times.
- … highlights/emphasises to the reader the importance of …
- … positions her readers to demand that they be informed about …
- … provokes a likely response from the reader …
- … encourages basketball fans to agree that …

- Voxi's repeated use of digital language may alienate readers who don't agree that the only way is …
- The extreme point of view presented by Gover is likely to polarise his audience as …
- Brown presents her key points logically and positions her audience of parents to consider the fairness of her points which, in turn, may result in their questioning of Principal Black's blanket ban.
- Voxi combines a conversational and confident tone with figurative and inclusive language, arguments, comparisons and popular examples to appeal to her audience of online readers who are 'digital savvy'.

Hint! Include the specific audience if known (e.g. 'basketball fans', 'parents', 'students' and 'teachers').

Structure terms and examples

- Local rapper, Jono D, begins his blog with …
- Voxi begins by stating …
- Opening his keynote speech with a collegial and inclusive salutation, 'Ladies and gentlemen', Lee immediately asserts …
- [Author's name] continues his argument …
- [Author's name] further describes
- The closing words, 'thank you' …
- McQueen finishes his article with [example].
- Professor Lee closes with a slide depicting …
- Day's blog invites commentary from her audience.
- In response to Carter's article, Dr Ambrose's email asserts that …
- In contrast to [author X's] call to action, [author Y] closes his speech with …
- The closing words, [example], remind the reader of their responsibility and are likely to lead to …
- In her final words, Fiona Carter acknowledges [example] unlike Palmer who …

Language to avoid

Use formal language. Don't write how you speak, or use shorthand or SMS language in your analysis. Avoid beginning sentences with 'Then', 'So'. Don't commentate, e.g. 'another example is…'

Avoid	Alternatives
Nolan starts off with [QUOTE] gives off the feeling that … all in all at the beginning In the next paragraph making parents relax off their kids cases brought upon puts forward comes across +	Nolan begins with [QUOTE] creates in conclusion initially subsequently encouraging parents to adopt a more relaxed approach provoked conveys to the reader suggests and
U This is an example of [technique] used by the writer. …makes her readers feel X puts the reader off when … pushes the point to gain the side of the parents the photo helps depict it to the reader makes the reader feel angry	You The writer uses [technique] such as [example] to appeal to … … encourages her readers to feel … X may alienate the reader when … emphasises the point that … to draw parents onside the photo highlights to the reader … likely to anger readers who feel strongly about social justice

Language analysis checklist

1 COAST is identified in introduction. ☐
2 Points and paragraphs are linked. ☐
3 Tone and tonal shifts are analysed. ☐
4 Key persuasive language and techniques are analysed. ☐
5 Lots of small relevant quotes are included. ☐
6 Key arguments/main points analysed. ☐
7 Visual analysis is woven through analysis. ☐
8 Clear and logical structure is used. ☐
9 Audience emotional appeals and position is included. ☐
10 Likely impact on target audience is included. ☐

PETs (Practical Editing Tips)

Stay in same tense

- Tense indicates time and action and is determined by verb endings and auxiliary verbs.
- There are three simple tenses: past, present and future.
- Verbs (main) are doing, being or having words, e.g. 'show', 'portray', 'own'.
- Auxiliary verbs include 'am', 'are', 'is', 'was', 'were', 'has', 'have'.
- Present tense works well for language analysis, e.g. 'contends', 'asserts'.

	Simple past tense	**Simple present tense**
Verbs (main)	portrayed, demonstrated, manipulated, created	emphasises, demonstrates, manipulates, positions
Auxiliary verbs	was, had, were, has	is, are, am

Use paragraphs

- Avoid writing one giant paragraph.
- Start a new paragraph for every main point, argument and emotion you analyse.
- Paragraphs can range from a few words to over a hundred words (provided the topic stays the same).
- Each paragraph should have a topic sentence at the start.
- Link your paragraphs using connectives (link word and phrases).
- Indent, justify or leave two lines between paragraphs.

Commas

- Commas make sentences easier to understand.
- Use commas before and after titles, e.g. Helen Day's popular blog, *Street Beat,* uses social media to discuss the changing attitudes towards tattoos.
- Commas are no longer used as separators in addresses or for dates (e.g. 16 May 2020).
- In language analysis you do not have to include commas before quotes, like you would in text responses.

Hint! Avoid long sentences with numerous commas.

Quoting rules for analysis

1. 'Quote fest.' Include lots of quotes to support points.
2. It's OK to quote in your introduction, i.e. quote part of contention if you can.

3 Avoid quoting big chunks of text.
4 Weave quotes of one or two words into your sentences, e.g. 'His last point exhorts parents to "be a good sport" and to "behave properly" before, during and after a game.'
5 Use quotation marks to show where a quote begins and finishes.
6 Underline titles of texts rather than quoting them. (This gives your writing a cleaner look.)
7 Single quotes are widely recommended, with double quotes used to quote within a quote, e.g. Ms Blackburn said, 'An easy way to "publish" is to create your own blog and post it'.

Formal language rules

1 Adopt a serious and polite tone.
2 Use paragraphs with topic sentences.
3 Check that spelling, punctuation and grammar are accurate.
4 Stay in the same tense.
5 Do not use contractions, e.g. 'can't', unless they are part of a quote.
6 Do not use slang or informal words, e.g. 'The writer is fed up with the government's crappy decisions.'
7 Do not write how you speak, e.g. begin sentences with 'So' or 'Then'.
8 Do not use visual language, e.g. 'It was a p*&^%$!!'.
9 Do not include your thoughts on an issue or argument in brackets, e.g. 'The PM (who looks weird as!) …'.
10 Use correct metalanguage (key terms).

Practice activities

1 Spelling exercise

Rewrite the following key analysis words, spelling them correctly.

exageration, arguement, oppinion, retorical, definately, writter, interprit, contraversial, mannor, biassed, beleef, 'The Herald Son', Currant affair, effectavely, justafy, sentance, plausable, indicitive, apauled, reffering, enviroment, existance, annidote, ultamitly, priveledge, representitive, reitterate, relaxment, agreeance, seperate, desperit, experiance, pursuade

2 Editing exercise

Practise your editing skills by identifying mistakes in the following examples from language analyses.

- So, Carter encourages her audience to protest against whaling by clicking on the 'Save the wail' petition icon.
- U see that the writer included lots of rhetorical Qs l8r in his piece.
- I don't agree that we should ban mobile phones in classrooms (no way never!)
- This is an example of the writer using appeals.
- Dr Ambrose puts the reader off when he goes on and on about gaming being bad for us. LOL.
- In her blog Fiona Carter puts across to her followers that public transport is too expensive (Amen to that).
- Mycroft includes visual language like drawings and stuff to come across as funny so that his audience will agree with him about pollies earning too much money.

3 Common mistakes

These pairs of words are often used incorrectly. Write definitions for and try to find a way of remembering which is which e.g. **affects (verb)** involves action while **effect** (nouns) is the end product.

- Affects/effects
- Compliment/complement
- Sympathy/empathy
- Immigrate/emigrate

4 Introduction audit

Examine the two sample introductions in this chapter and identify:

- contention
- contention verbs
- outline sentences
- target audience
- form
- language style
- tone.

5 Language analysis practice

Practise writing language analyses for the following exams and adapted exams. Write under timed conditions.

- *Chickens Range Free?* [VCAA 2008 sample English exam, modified]
- *Are we Overprotected?* [VCAA 2007 English exam, modified]
- *Mobiles Immobilised* [VCAA 2004 English exam, adapted]
- *A Word from our Coach* **...** [VCAA 2008 English exam]
- *Keyed In* [VCAA 2009 English exam]
- *Taking Stock* [VCAA 2010 English exam]

- *FINished with Fins*
- *The Power of Ink* [VCAA 2011 English Exam]

Some suggested responses for VCAA exams 2008, 2009, 2010 and 2011 can be found in Chapter 8.

1 *Chickens Range Free?* [VCAA 2008 sample English exam, modified]

MAINSTREAM: TASK
How is written and visual language used to attempt to persuade readers to share the point of view of the writer of *Chickens Range Free*?

EAL TASK: Part 1
Write a note-form summary of the text, *Chickens Range Free?*

EAL TASK: Part 2
Write a piece of prose that explains how language and visual features have been used in *Chickens Range Free?* to attempt to persuade readers about three of the main points in the opinion page of the newspaper and letter to the editor.

Background information
This opinion piece, with the accompanying photograph, and letter to the editor were published on a website and on the 'Opinion' page of a Melbourne newspaper.

It was written in response to a recent incident in a Melbourne suburb during which hundreds of chickens were illegally released from cages on a truck. The truck was on its way from a poultry farm to a meat-processing factory.
The police said that some of the chickens were run over by passing traffic and others disappeared into nearby backyards and parkland.

Onlookers saw two people leaving the scene, but only one person has been apprehended so far. The farmer has declared that he would sue the culprits, whether or not they are charged in the courts. Poultry farmer, Simon Brand, wrote a response to the article.

Opinion, January 2007

Chickens Range Free?

Drawing attention to the rights of oppressed animals expands our understanding of the rights of humans as well, writes Jo Smith.

Last week a truck was intercepted by activists and hundreds of chickens were given their freedom. I wasn't involved in the liberation, but as a member of Australians for Animal Rights (AAR) I understand completely why the action was taken. Direct action is the only way to bring the public's attention to the dire plight of the oppressed animals on this planet. Some people may think that liberating a truckload of chickens is too drastic a measure, but I think the activists risked life and limb for a noble cause. It is important for someone to stand up for the rights of animals. Since the incident, the local media have fallen over themselves to give air time to critics of the action. A man who was walking his dog nearby at the time of the incident reportedly said: 'It's a wonder someone wasn't hurt. These activists have a lot to answer for.' A talk-back radio presenter began his show the next morning by sneering: 'Fancy a free-range chicken?' He went on to refer to the action as 'nonsense', the activists as 'idiotic ... clowns' and 'anti-social hippies and bludgers', and to whip up his listeners into a frenzy of support for the 'poor farmer'.

However, we Australians for Animal Rights believe that all animals deserve to be free to lead natural lives. We believe, as humans, we are not only doing the animals an injustice when we mistreat them, but that we are also doing ourselves an injustice. We have overpopulated the planet and drastically decreased the numbers of animal species. We treat so-called 'farm animals' in abominably cruel ways, to provide cheap food when we could afford to pay more. When humans condone abusing other species for self-serving purposes, surely it is but a short step to condoning widespread human rights abuses? It is little wonder that compassionate people resort to extreme action.

Too many people have a simplistic human-centred view of the world. We must reform this attitude to our fellow inhabitants of the earth, our furred and feathered friends. Animals have the same rights as we do to breathe fresh, clean air and to live in comfortable, healthy conditions.

AAR does not believe it is 'antisocial' to liberate animals from inhumane conditions. Being trapped in cages only 450 square centimetres in size, unable to move, and without proper ventilation are inhumane conditions. Chickens are possibly the most abused animals on the face of the earth, treated so badly that if the public knew the details of how they lived and died, few would go on eating them.

The philosopher Jeremy Bentham once said, 'The question is not, can they reason? Nor, can they talk? But, can they suffer?' If only more people would realise that animals, as sentient beings like us, have rights that should be respected, then perhaps humans would become more humane in their treatment of one another – that is, we would better understand human rights!

Until a humane alternative to keeping hens in inhumane conditions can be found, an action which frees caged chickens is justified, no matter what damage may have been caused. Because animal rights is such an important issue, breaking the law to free those poor creatures last week was justified. In this case, the end definitely justified the means!

Jo Smith is a freelance writer and publicity officer for Australians for Animal Rights.

Whose rights?

I have been a poultry farmer for twenty years. The activists who set upon the driver did not 'free' or 'liberate' chickens. They committed an illegal act for which they will be charged and have to face our legal system. They put the driver and other motorists at risk. They have cost the farmer thousands of dollars in lost income. Activists of any sort, whether they belong to Greenpeace, PETA or AAR have the right to protest legally. However when they indulge in illegal protests that result in property damage or risk human life they have become criminals. Poultry farming is not illegal. Eating chicken is not illegal. Us poultry farmers have a right to be able to deliver our product to the market. Attacking a truck and stealing chickens is illegal.

Simon Brand, Tooradin.

2 Are we overprotected? [VCAA 2007 English exam, modified]

MAINSTREAM: TASK
How is written and visual language used to attempt to persuade readers to share the point of view in the texts, *Overprotective parents stifle growth* and *Reality Check* and the accompanying visual on the 'Opinion' page?

EAL TASK: Part 1
Write a note-form summary of the text.

EAL TASK: Part 2
Write a piece of prose that explains how language and visual features have been used by the writer in an attempt to persuade readers about three of the main points in the two letters and photograph on the 'Opinion' page.

Are we overprotected?
Parenting styles have changed over the years and much has been written about the best way to bring up children. Some experts advise new parents to implement a regime of strict control and rigid routine for their children's own protection. Others argue for a more permissive, liberal style of parenting to encourage children to be independent and become more resilient adults. This pattern continues into adulthood. Laws intended to protect people could be seen to prevent them from taking personal responsibility for their own actions.

The following material presents a range of viewpoints on this issue.

The Daily News Friday 19 October 2007

OPINION PAGE

Overprotective parents stifle growth

How much longer will we continue to supposedly 'protect' our young people from the stark realities of life? It is perfectly clear to me, as a professional, that by mollycoddling them, we are ultimately creating defenceless young people unable to cope with future challenges.

Too often are parents willing to step in and stand up for their 'perfect' children involved in 'incidents' at school, or caught up in squabbles with their peers. Parents provide a continuous taxi service, transporting their previous offspring to organised sporting activities, to and from school, often running little errands for them. They blindly search for the child's lost jumper and they obediently bring the lunch when it is forgotten. Others even complete their children's homework.

One only has to look at teenagers today: incapable of making a decision on their own; followers, not leaders; still reliant on their parents for their creature comforts. Children need to make mistakes, experience rejection and maybe hurt themselves to learn how to cope with life. They must experience real pain and deal with disappointment to become resilient adults.

Nothing could be clearer to me than the belief that, by wrapping our children in cotton wool, we are depriving them of the skills required to solve the problems which they will confront in the future. They cannot possibly learn to deal with challenging situations in adulthood if they never have to face a problem in youth.

Parents are so afraid their children will be hurt or abducted that they are refusing to let them play outside on their own until they are at least 14, research has revealed. Denied opportunities to meet friends, a generation of cosseted youngsters is becoming lonely and isolated, according to a study by the Children's Society in Britain.

The Children's Society stresses the importance of allowing children freedom to play with peers as it helps them 'practise making and consolidating friendships and deal with conflict'. Children who are isolated from peers are at greater risk of becoming depressed, overaggressive, antisocial and delinquent, they argue.

There is a mountain of evidence available now to show that children whose parents are at their constant beck and call are stifled, losing the ability to develop the skills to become fully functioning adults. Furthermore, they never accept responsibility for their own actions.

Jane Brown
Retired Principal

A reader has his say

REALITY CHECK

My grandad goes on about the good old days. He says that in his time kids could be kids. They were not hassled by parents and if they jolly well wanted to play in the street till dark, they jolly well did.

I used to actually believe this, but not now. Now I have my own family and I love my kids. The world has changed and it's weird.

I say unsupervised is unsafe!

Everywhere I turn, I see danger.

Cars are lethal weapons with hoons at the wheel. Newspapers scream stories of tragedy and evil. Even in our very own family room there is no escape. The News at 6 means that we are bombarded with scenes of carnage caused by suicide bombers wherever the bloodiest massacre of the last 24 hours has occurred.

If it's not that, it's films filled with foul language, violence or 'adult themes'. Even the Internet lures young people into sampling the 'thrill' of life in the fast lane.

It terrifies me.

Don't try the documentaries either. They are full of gloom and doom about climate change, mass extinctions and death of the planet.

Don't tell me that kids should be allowed to see all this. What does it do to them?

I want my kids to be able to survive in this crazy world, and to do that they need to be safe and secure and sure of some things – things like love and hope. They need to feel that they can make a difference.

That won't happen if they are traumatised – or worse!

Jack Lee

HANDLE
WITH CARE
IS SOCIETY RAISING
A GENERATION
OF SOOKS?

3 Mobiles Immobilised [VCAA 2004 English exam, modified]

MAINSTREAM: TASK
How is written and visual language used to attempt to persuade readers to share the points of view of Principal John Black and parent May Brown?

EAL TASK: Part 1
Write a note-form summary of Principal Black's message and May Brown's letter and sign.

EAL TASK: Part 2
Write a piece of prose that explains how language and visual features have been used in the principal's message and a letter from a parent with an accompanying sign to attempt to persuade readers about three of the main points in the texts.

Background information
In his message in the newsletter for parents, Principal Black from Metro High School announced a complete ban on students bringing mobile phones to school.

In response to the ban, May Brown, a parent, wrote a letter with an accompanying suggested sign.

Principal's message in the parent newsletter

Parent News **Wednesday**
Metro High School **12 May 2004**

MHS Excellence

Message from the Principal

Many of you will remember the article in last October's *Parent News* which described the problems caused by students bringing mobile phones to school. School Council discussed the issue again last night. It has been decided that **no student will be allowed to bring a mobile phone onto school property**. Any mobile phone brought to school will be removed from the student's possession. Naturally, the student will receive an automatic detention.

The key reasons that this decision has been made are as follows:

- Classes are being severely disrupted by students who insist on hiding mobile phones and bringing them into class.
- Obsessive text messaging in particular seems to be a pastime which distracts students from their work.
- There are concerns about security in tests and examinations. A number of distressing examples have occurred recently. Students have attempted to cheat using mobile phones. These, they claimed, were needed for 'emergencies'.
- So far this year no fewer than 37 students have claimed that phones have been stolen from lockers or bags. Others have been 'lost'.
- The introduction of phones with cameras has led to some particularly unsavoury incidents. No fewer than three times this year phones have been left on 'accidentally' in changing rooms.

This decision will not be popular with some people. Some will say that their rights are being violated. Every sensible person, however, will agree that the interests of the community must take precedence over the selfish desires of individuals. The values of this educational institution must be upheld. The focus of this school on education and responsibility must be preserved.

John Black
Principal
Metro High School

Figure 4.4
PRINCIPAL'S MESSAGE IN THE PARENT NEWSLETTER FROM 2004 VCAA ENGLISH EXAM

14 Stone Street
Metro
21 May

Dear Mr Black

I was very upset when I first read about your blanket ban on students bringing mobile phones to school. I am still really upset. To outlaw the mobile phone is to deny students and parents the use of technology that has made our lives simpler and safer.

When we decided to buy a mobile phone for our daughter two years ago it made life so much easier for us. Both my husband and I are in the workforce and we can never be sure when we will arrive home from work. Our daughter travels by public transport which, as you know, is notoriously unreliable. She comes home at different times and we really need to know what time she will be leaving to come home each day. Furthermore, as you know, she has a medical condition which makes it important for her to be able to contact us during the day.

What's more, it seems to us, rules like this don't help educate our children. It is not good educational practice. Some students are misusing their phones so all students are to be penalised! When adults break laws, we have to suffer the consequences. As responsible, mature citizens we've learned, perhaps through making mistakes, to act considerately. I'd have though that self-discipline was the key to a truly harmonious community.

Furthermore, wouldn't it have been a good idea for students to play a role in setting the rules that they would then be more likely to keep? School should build true individual responsibility in students. Our community as a whole may benefit from this in the long run.

I can appreciate your irritation when students break rules, but please reconsider your decision.

Yours sincerely

May Brown
Parent

4 *A word from our coach* … [VCAA 2008 English exam]

MAINSTREAM: TASK
How is written and visual language used to attempt to persuade readers to share the point of view of the writer of *A word from our coach …?*

EAL TASK: Part 1
Write a note-form summary of the text *A word from our coach …?*

EAL TASK: Part 2
Write a piece of prose that explains how language and visual features have been used in *A word from our coach …?* to attempt to persuade readers about three of the main points in the online article.

Background information
The following newsletter was distributed to the parents and supporters of a local sports club at the commencement of a new season.

The column was written in response to concerns about the poor behaviour of spectators in the previous season and the increased difficulty of attracting volunteers to the club.

Local Sports Club

Club News

Volume 1, Issue 1

A word from our coach ...

Emily was distraught when the netball game staggered to an end. She didn't care that her beloved team had lost. She didn't care about her own performance. She didn't care about the sledging by the other team. She cared desperately that her dad had yelled at her – in front of all her team-mates – for failing to shoot the goal and save the game. Emily is just 8 years old.

Sportsmanship: play fair

Toxic parents are poisoning our club. They're not the parents we want: the ones who forget that the only goal that should matter in kids' sport is the promotion of good sportsmanship.

What sort of parent are you?

What is good sportsmanship?

Good sportsmanship occurs when team-mates, opponents, coaches and officials treat each other with respect. Children learn the fundamentals of true sportsmanship from the adults in their lives, especially their parents. Young people who see adults behaving in a sportsmanlike way come to understand that the real winners in sport are those who know how to persevere and to behave with dignity – whether they win or lose a game. Their heroism comes from their ability to cheerfully rebound from a loss, striving constantly for self-improvement and physical excellence.

We all remember that Olympic runner who stopped to help his rival who had fallen over. *That* was truly heroic.

I know all our parents help their children to understand that good sportsmanship includes both small gestures and heroic efforts. It starts with something as simple as shaking hands with opponents before a game and includes applauding good play made by others and accepting bad umpiring calls gracefully. Displaying good sportsmanship isn't always easy; it can be truly tough to congratulate the opposing team after losing a hard-fought, close or important game. But the young people who learn how to do it will benefit in many, many ways. It will be a triumph of the human spirit.

Isn't good sportsmanship a model for life?

Be reasonable

Some clubs have coaches who only care about winning and even yell abuse at their own team members who get so scared that they think it's OK to be ruthless on the field. Last year we saw parents at our club have the same negative effect. And they were banned from attending matches. When this happened many of our hard-working volunteers left our club disgusted by the parents' behaviour.

Why waste our Saturdays with louts like these? Faced with sports rage, good parents won't come any more and coaches will hang up their whistles.

We don't want a repetition of this stuff round here. There's enough to cope with in running junior sport. If you want to have a go at anyone, have a go at me. Don't take it out on the kids.

Be a good sport

So when does winning take over from the thrill of just being part of the team? At what age do kids forget to just have fun? Parents have a responsibility to show their kids what appropriate behaviour is before, during and after the game.

Adults who emphasise good sportsmanship see winning as just one of several goals they'd like their kids to achieve. They help young athletes take pride in their accomplishments and in their improving skills, so that kids see themselves as winners, even if the scoreboard doesn't show the numbers going in their favour.

The best coaches – and parents – encourage their kids to play fair, to have fun, and to concentrate on helping the team while at the same time polishing their own skills.

Remember the saying 'Actions speak louder than words'? That's especially true when it comes to teaching your kids the basics of good sportsmanship. Your behaviour during practices and games will influence them more than any pep talk or lecture you or I give them.

Coach Sam

5 Keyed In [VCAA 2009 English exam]

MAINSTREAM: TASK
How is written and visual language used to attempt to persuade readers to share the point of view of the writer of *Keyed In*?

EAL TASK: Part 1
Write a note-form summary of the article, *Keyed In*, found below.

EAL TASK: Part 2
Write a piece of prose that explains how language and visual features have been used in *Keyed In* to attempt to persuade readers about three of the main points in the online article.

Background information
The following opinion piece appeared in *Ctrl Alt,* an online journal. It was posted earlier this year in response to the increasing debate about the impact of digital technology.

Digital Technology > Voxi >> **Keyed In**

23 May 2009

Keyed In
New ways of doing things always tend to polarize people. Some people are naturally afraid of the new, challenged by the discomfort of being dislodged from the known, the safe, the predictable, the true and the tested – in short, their comfort zone. They take the view, 'if it works, why fix it?' And maybe they have a point – sometimes it's good to take time out and just enjoy what you've got.

Other people are fired up by new things. They're excited by the possibility of the unknown; the further horizons and the expanding universe really do it for them. They want to grab the future with both hands and make it happen. They see possibilities for making things better where other people want to chill, just responding to the pleasure of the moment.

History's full of moments though, when human beings have been moved forward by people who have been like the grit in an oyster. Gritty people produce pearls. Well, sort of. They're the ones who ask questions, who tinker away in the garage, who turn up on 'The Inventors'.

In our lifetime we haven't had a Copernicus or Galileo reorganizing the cosmos, or a Darwin challenging us with a radically new theory of evolution. In a way, what we do have, though, is something that in time may prove even more dramatic for humankind than the development of writing or printing was.

Out of a garage in the United States has come digital technology – a discovery that is already revolutionizing human experience and the way we live our lives together in the world. Just as the microscope opened up new worlds, and the telescope let us look at ones that we hadn't seen so well before, digital technology has revolutionized the way we communicate with each other and is also promising to revolutionise the way we learn and think. This is a fundamental challenge to some people who fear that our humanity will be diminished. Some fear this will reduce human intelligence, replace human memory, displace cognitive function with an increasingly sophisticated artificial intelligence. For instance, this is what I got from a podcast:

> ' … the digital world is a world of the here and now, a world of the sound byte, a world of an instant frozen moment where nothing has consequences, and where everything is literal. Where nothing has a meaning. You're not saying one thing in terms of something else, you're saying, literally what you see is what you get … The brain is what we call plastic … and because of this so-called plasticity … every moment you're alive it's modified and changed and revised every little experience, literally leaving a mark on your brain.'

Others can appreciate that by connecting digital technology and the human brain, human beings can become even more intelligent, faster than evolution alone allows. *Homo sapiens*, who succeeded *homo habilis,* might just become *homo supersapiens.* The adventurous will want to see whether that can happen, will want to know where we can go, whether we can evolve in such a way that we can solve the riddles of the universe, find cures faster, find ways of preserving the planet, ending war and violence, feeding the teeming multitudes and ensuring that people everywhere have the opportunity to lead happy, safe and fulfilling lives in a free and peaceful world. OK, it's a dream – but we need dreams as well as this digital technology, the exciting tool of the modern world. Why wouldn't you want it in your life?

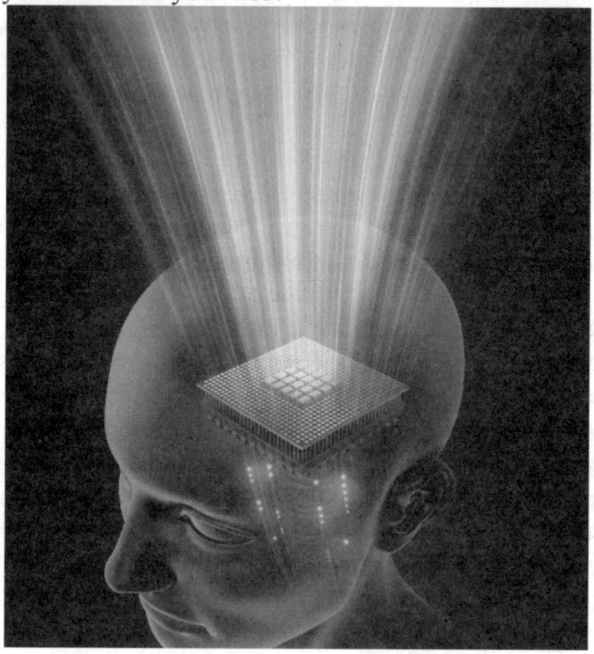

The impact of that technology on us, the way it has the power to change the way we think, the potential it offers to us for enhancing our lives: these are things which people of our generation just accept and use with enthusiasm. It's older people who are less familiar with it who are suspicious about it, or even afraid. What's to be afraid of? Our minds take in information the way the Net distributes it: in a swiftly moving stream of particles. Once scuba divers drowning in a sea of words, we now zip along the surface like jet skiers.

Global shopping, online banking, working out the itinerary for your holiday, looking up Google Maps and Street View to check out where your friends live, and that's not to mention Facebook and keeping in touch and keeping up: these are fantastic advantages which have already proved themselves. Sure, some people stress about privacy issues, but these can be resolved. Google is not allowed to film defence sites from Google cars and Google bikes. Let's face it; the pictures we see are not real-time images. You can protest about them anyway and get them removed or pixelated if you're really worried. Besides, the hot air balloons are always hovering over my back yard and looking into my windows too.

Why go to a library when you can sit at your desk and look up Wikipedia or Google Scholar, or Ask Jeeves? Besides, people who wouldn't normally go to a library actually do that – that's a win.

If people stopped learning tables and using log books when calculators came in, then that's because something better turned up. They didn't stop using their brains; they just used their brains for different things, like inventing the Net!

Let's be excited – keep being excited. We'd still be swinging in the trees or huddling in caves if we'd taken the view that new things are harmful or dangerous or unpredictable. The ever-expanding Googleness of the universe means that we're better informed, know more about each other, can push back the boundaries of darkness and ignorance and like the people who struck rocks together and found the magic of a spark, and then learned how to repeat and use that experience or discovery, people who are digital savvy, and aren't we all, are heading for the 22nd century in a spirit of optimism. Bring it on, I say. If you don't agree, you can always put your computer on eBay and buy a stack of stationery with the money, if that's your thing, but what a loser you'd be. Like wireless, it's about getting faster and more efficient, being in touch and connected. The future is here now, and I pretty much like the look of it.

Voxi

6 Taking Stock [VCAA 2010 English exam]

SECTION C – Analysis of language use (Using language to persuade)

Instructions for Section C

Section C requires students to analyse the ways in which language and visual features are used to present a point of view.

Section C is worth one-third of the total assessment for the examination. Read the speech *Taking Stock* and then complete the task below.

Write your analysis as a coherently structured piece of prose.

MAINSTREAM: TASK

How is written and visual language used to attempt to persuade the audience to share the point of view of the speaker in his speech *Taking Stock*?

EAL TASK: Part 1
Write a note-form summary of the speech, *Taking Stock.* Your response must be in **note form.** Do not use complete sentences.

EAL TASK: Part 2
Write a piece of prose that explains how language and visual features have been used in *Taking Stock* to attempt to persuade the audience about three of the main points in the speech.

> **Background information**
> Biodiversity is the term used to describe life on Earth – the variety of living things, the places they inhabit and the interactions between them.
>
> The transcript of the keynote speech given by Professor Chris Lee at the International Biodiversity Conference 2010 held in Nagoya, Japan, from 25 to 27 October is printed here.

In 2002 a commitment was made to achieve 'a significant reduction in the rate of biodiversity loss as a contribution to poverty alleviation and to the benefit of all life on earth' by 2010. The purpose of this Nagoya conference was to review progress towards achieving the target and to look beyond 2010.

Opening slide of speaker's presentation

Ladies and gentlemen,

This is a year of vital significance to our world. In declaring 2010 to be the International Year of Biodiversity, the United Nations stated: 'It is a celebration of life on earth and of the value of biodiversity in our lives. The world is invited to take action in 2010 to safeguard the variety of life on earth: biodiversity.'

Has this been a year of celebration of life on earth? Has this, in fact, been a year of action?

Eight years ago – in April 2002 – many of our countries made a commitment to achieve a significant reduction in the rate of biodiversity loss. Over the next two days we will be reviewing our progress in this area. Honestly, how well have we done?

It is with great pleasure – though not without a tinge of sadness – that I address you on this occasion and work with you to re-establish, indeed to strengthen, our goals for the next decade.

One may justly ask: how far have we really come in our commitment to achieve a significant reduction in the rate of biodiversity loss as a contribution to poverty alleviation and to ensure the preservation of life on earth? For, perhaps idealistically, this is *exactly* what we set out to do.

Sadly, over the last one hundred years, we have lost 35% of mangroves, 40% of forests and 50% of wetlands. Due to our own thoughtless human actions, species are being lost at a rate that is estimated to be up to 100 times the natural rate of extinction. Of the IUCN (International Union for Conservation of Nature) Red List of 44837 species assessed, 38% are today threatened and 804 already extinct. It is too late for them.

In truth, for the first time since the dinosaurs disappeared, animals and plants are being driven towards extinction faster than new species can evolve. We are in the grip of a species extinction being driven by the destruction of natural habitats, hunting, the spread of alien predators, disease and climate change. Reversing this negative trend is not only possible, but essential to human wellbeing.

We know this. We are, in truth, the most educated generation of any to date. We have no excuse for inaction. Clearly it is our lack of unity and lack of genuine commitment to action that have led us to this grim situation.

For too long our approach has been haphazard. Wonderful words, glossy brochures, inspiring documentaries are no substitute for real action. It is one thing to mouth platitudes in the comfort of an air conditioned and sumptuously catered conference hall and quite another to produce concrete results. A zoo here, a national park there, faint promises at conferences such as ours, a talk-fest of targets. What have WE – what have YOU and YOUR country – actually done since 2002 to contribute to the achievement of our goals?

There is no need to remind you why biological diversity is so important. As we all well know, our failure to conserve and use biological diversity in a sustainable manner is resulting in environmental degradation, new and more rampant illnesses, deepening poverty and a continuing pattern of inequitable and untenable growth on a global scale. Healthy ecosystems are vital to regulating the global climate. Poor rural communities depend on biodiversity for health and nutrition, for crop development, and as a safety net when faced with climate variability and natural disasters. Indeed, the poor are particularly vulnerable because they are directly dependent on biodiversity for their very survival, yet they are not in a position to do anything about it.

Species diversity affects the quantity and quality of human food supply. Biodiversity loss undermines the food security, nutrition and health of the rural poor and even increases their vulnerability. More than 1.1 billion people remain in extreme poverty and, while the wellbeing of all people is dependent on ecosystem services, it is the dependence of the poor on these services which is most crucial. Poverty eradication is crucial to a global action plan, yet the needs of the poor are often subordinated to the interests of us, the powerful economic giants. It is time we stopped kidding ourselves that the epidemic of affluenza is having little effect upon fragile ecosystems across our planet. We affluent hunters and gatherers must hunt less, gather less, conserve more and preserve more before it is too late!

Is any of this new information? Of course not! As leaders in the area of biodiversity, we know what damage our lifestyle is doing to our world. The time for talk is over: now, truly, is the time for serious action. We must reinforce this message to those in power: to the politicians, to the corporate leaders, even to the everyday householder.

I leave you with the words of the ecologist Thomas Eisner: 'Biodiversity is the greatest treasure we have … Its diminishment is to be prevented at all costs'.

Thank you.

Closing slide of speaker's presentation

7 FINished with fins

TASK

How is written and visual language used to attempt to persuade the audience to share the points of view in the article, *FINished with fins*, and the response?

Background information

- On June 26 OZSTAR announced that it would carry shark products only from sustainable sources on its flights in the future. The ban follows a year-long campaign by some 60 environmental groups in Hong Kong to stop shark fin being flown into the city.
- The following contains an article with an accompanying image from the national newspaper, *Daily Courier,* by Sam McQueen, a lecturer in Sustainability and Marine Ecosystems from Clyde University, Queensland. The article includes one image.
- It also contains a letter in response to the article by A Ziffel.

FINished with fins

Yesterday OZSTAR, like Ocean Pacific and Maji Airlines, announced that it would carry shark products only from sustainable sources on its flights in the future. The ban follows a year-long campaign by some 60 environmental groups in Hong Kong to stop shark fin being flown into the city. Hong Kong handles at least fifty percent of the word trade in shark fin with more than 10,300 tonnes of shark fin imported to Hong Kong last year.

Shark fin soup is traditionally served at formal occasions in Chinese culture to symbolise both the wealth of the host and respect for their guests. With an increasingly affluent Chinese middle class, the demand for shark fin soup is driving a five annual increase in the shark fin trade, putting additional pressure on a range of shark species, many of which are already considered endangered.

With a single shark fin up for sale for $1000 in Sydney or Melbourne's Chinatown, it's not hard to see the incentive for shark fishing. Prices can reach up to $700 per kg of dried, skinless fin, whereas shark meat is generally much lower value – selling for as little as $0.80 per kg.

Live shark finning is the barbaric practice of cutting off a shark's fins then throwing the living shark back into the ocean. When the living shark is returned to the ocean minus its fins it must swim constantly in order to breathe. Unable to move effectively it sinks to the bottom where it dies of suffocation or is eaten by other predators.

Shark finning has increased over the past decade largely due to the increased demand for shark fin soup and traditional cures, particularly in China. Nearly every fin of a shark is targeted for harvest. This practice, illegal and legal, is seriously threatening the global shark population.

Live shark finning is illegal. Australian legislation, like many other countries, dictates that all sharks caught must be from a ‘sustainable shoal’ and ‘landed’ i.e. sharks brought back to shore and fins harvested after death. However, legislation in Australia differs between various states, the Territory and the Commonwealth; in Commonwealth, NSW and Victorian waters, all sharks caught must be brought back to port (‘landed’) with their fins attached to their bodies. In Tasmanian, Western Australian, Northern Territory and Queensland waters however, fishers can cut the fins off at sea, as long as they bring back a ratio of shark fins to shark meat. This patchwork of shark processing across the country is a mess, and makes monitoring whether fishers are complying with shark finning legislation a nightmare, a fact recently recognised in an international forum.

Australian Marine Conservation Society explains that ‘Sustainable shoal’ is not just about the numbers of fish left in our oceans, it’s also the way in which fish are caught and the impact on the sea floor and marine ecosystems.

Air Kiwi and Soul-time Air airlines have announced blanket bans on the carriage of shark fins.

Alistair Kinnear, executive director of Ourocean and instigator of the campaign to stop shark fin arriving by air, said, ‘We applaud these airlines that have installed a blanket ban on shark fin. The truth is that shark finning is not sustainable and most catches cannot be verified.’

Why is Australia lagging behind? We need to announce a total ban as well.

Sharks grow slowly, reach maturity at a larger size and a later age, and have low reproductive rates. Like whales, they are especially vulnerable to overfishing methods, such as shark finning. This can have a dire effect on our marine eco systems, particularly coral reefs, as sharks play an important role at the top of the marine food chain.

Studies estimate that 26–73 million sharks are harvested annually for their fins.

According to the Australian Marine Conservation Society shark finning has increased by 5% annually. Numbers of some shark species have dropped as much as 80% over the last fifty years.

Australia and OZSTAR are complicit in driving our global shark populations closer to extinction by our role in the international shark fin trade.

It's a simple matter of demand and supply. If we remove the supply and we will decrease the demand. The Australian Government needs to ban both the import and export of shark fin. A ban on the trade will serve to ensure sharks aren't fished for the value of their fins, and reduce the incentives for shark fishing across the country.

If we want to preserve our marine ecosystems we can and need to do more!

If you want to help protect sharks and their fins from ending up in a bowl of soup:

- access www.ourocean.org and sign the petition
- walk out of restaurants that serve shark fin soup
- support airlines that have a blanket ban on shark fins.

Sam McQueen. Lecturer in Sustainability and Marine Ecosystems
smcqueen@clydeuni.qld.edu.au

Sharks are killers!
While I've never eaten shark fin soup or taken any shark cures, I respect other countries' traditions and cultures. Sharks are not like whales. Sharks are predators – pure and simple. They are known as 'apex predators' or top level predators. Sharks are at the top of their food chain and we are on their menu! The International Shark Attack File (ISAF) has Australia ranked highest in terms of shark fatalities. In 2008 alone there were 48 shark attacks in Australia with 11 fatalities.
Watch Jaws!
A. Ziffle

VCAA 2011 English exams

Section C – Analysis of language use

Language analysis is only Section C.

Instructions for Section C

Section C requires students to analyse the ways in which language and visual features are used to present a point of view.

Section C is worth one-third of the total assessment for the examination.

Read all parts of the blog ***The Power of Ink*** and then complete the task below.

Write your analysis as a coherently structured piece of prose.

Your response will be assessed according to the criteria set out in this book.

TASK

How is written and visual language used to attempt to persuade the audience to share the points of view in the online blog *Street Beat*?

Background information

Helen Day is a part-time journalist and blogger. She maintains her blog entitled *Street Beat* in which she comments on a variety of current social issues. This blog entry, *The Power of Ink*, is about tattoos and it has drawn a variety of responses from readers of her blog.

The Power of Ink

FRIDAY 25 MARCH 2011

Once a sign of deviance and criminality, they're now a fashion statement.

Everyone has tattoos these days: even me. I live near a mega shopping centre and every time I visit, I see enough ink on suburban housewives to outdo the collection in any Australian prison.

Since newsreaders, sitcom stars and upmarket shoppers began to draw roses, skulls, and Latin phrases on their flesh, the power of ink has diminished. The deviant nature of the tattoo has faded like, well a tattoo.

FOLLOWERS

There are **12,615** followers

Ta Moko is a Maori body art practice which shows that the wearer has status within the community. Ta Moko can also tell the story of the wearer's family heritage.

It was not always so.

From the earliest times, tattoos almost always meant trouble. First the Greeks and then the Romans inked the unconsenting backs of prisoners and slaves. The practice continued in Europe throughout the Middle Ages to mark the deviant and the incarcerated.

The indelible cruelty of the prison tattoo can still be seen living in the flesh of those who survived the concentration camps of World War II. There is little that suggests the horror of this genocide more than these numbered tattoos. For millennia, and with few exceptions, ink on the body signified ownership and brutality. These tattoos were an indication of control, a sign that the bearer had a value that hovered somewhere between property and machine.

No tattoos before you're thirty. What I'll tell my children…
Sam de Brito
Published by Penguin Australia, 2006

When something is imposed without our consent, we tend to develop a strong sense of satire. From at least the 18th

BLOG ARCHIVE
□ ▼ 2011 (41)
O▼ March (19)

ABOUT ME
Helen Day

century, those who had been marked by the State as 'deviant' began to create their own tattoos.

Convicts were known to mock the King by having the words, 'Property of Mother England' etched into the flesh on their backs. By these means, those who flogged them were reminded that they were vandalizing the property of the Crown.

In the 20th century, those traditions of defiance persisted. IN the 1990s, tattoo artists set up shop in every Australian shopping strip. And it was in one of these new body modification boutiques that I and many other young women, dared to 'defile' our femininity. Back then, a handful of us angry young things had symbols of our gender affixed to our own bodies. Tattoos have now become sexy and even adorn the ankle of the British Prime Minister's wife! Personally, I find this profoundly annoying. Here I am stuck not with a real memory of my feminist youth but an indelible kinship to Britain.

The tattoo has been commodified and now performs, more or less, as it originally did; it is fashion's proprietary mark. It's difficult of course to imagine a time when a tattoo marked anyone, man or woman, as a try hard. For a brief moment, however, I did feel the reckless abandon of Carnevale* unfolding on my skin. And now, I look at the symbol of my rebellion and I see an ornament as ordinary as any other cosmetic quirk.

*Carnevale – a Venetian festival at which people wear costumes and masks which conceal their identities.

Post a comment

Hey. Yea, I've got a tatt and I'm no nerd! My mum was rapt when I got mine and wanted one too. Some people still think that tatts are low life or for alternatives. No way!

I didn't just go to one of those sleazy places, not just anywhere. I designed my own ankle bracelet. No one else has one like mine. I'm unique! I had it done like at a tattoo art studio. And yeah, I do cross my legs so I can show it off.
Tash: 25 March 11.43 pm

Medical practitioners like me will tell you tattoos breach the skin which means that skin infections and other complications are possible. A tattoo is a permanent body mark on your skin with pigments inserted through small holes in the skin's top layer. The tattooist uses a hand-held machine that acts like a sewing machine with one or more needles piercing the skin repeatedly. With every puncture the needle inserts tiny ink droplets. The process, which is done without anaesthetic and may last several hours, can cause bleeding, hepatitis B, hepatitis C, tetanus, potentially significant pain, and a pus-like drainage.
Dr AB: 26 March 7.40 am

So many dolphin tattoos have faded and stretched into whales ... If you wouldn't put the picture on your wall, why pay some hack to needle it into your body? I'm a rebel and an individual – I have no tattoos!
Cleanskin: 26 March 7.53 am

Ta Moko is similar to an identity card. It is a sacred form of family and personal identification. They say that 'imitation is the sincerest form of flattery'. However, Ta Moko imitation is nothing less than identity theft. It's disgraceful and immoral. Ta Moko is as unique to the wearer as your own fingerprints. How would you feel if someone stole those from you?
Kiwi: 26 March 8.02 am

Examination assessment criteria

The examination will address all the criteria. All student responses will be assessed against each criterion. The extent to which the response is characterised by:

Section C – Analysis of language use (Using language to persuade)

- understanding of ideas and points of view presented
- analysis of ways in which language and visual features are used to present a point of view and to persuade readers
- controlled and effective use of language appropriate to the task

EAL Section C – Analysis of language use

Language analysis is only Section C.

Instructions for Section C

Section C consists of **two** parts.

Parts 1 and 2 are equally weighted.

Section C is worth 30 marks.

Carefully read the blog ***Tattoos: The Power of Ink*** and then complete **both** parts.

Your response will be assessed according to the criteria set out in this book.

TASK

Part 1

Write a note-form summary of the blog ***Tattoos: The Power of Ink*** found below. Your response must be in **note form**. Do not use complete sentences.

Part 2

Write a piece of prose that explains how language and visual features have been used in ***Tattoos: The Power of Ink*** to attempt to persuade the audience about three of the main points in the blog.

Background information
Helen Day is a part-time journalist and blogger. She maintains her blog entitled *Street Beat* in which she comments on a variety of current social issues. This blog entry, *The Power of Ink*, is about tattoos and it has drawn a variety of responses from readers of her blog.

The Power of Ink

FRIDAY 25 MARCH 2011

Once a sign of deviance and criminality, they're now a fashion statement.

Everyone has tattoos these days: even me. I live near a mega shopping centre and every time I visit, I see enough ink on suburban housewives to outdo the collection in any Australian prison.

Since newsreaders, sitcom stars and upmarket shoppers began to draw roses, skulls, and Latin phrases on their flesh, the power of ink has diminished. The deviant nature of the tattoo has faded like, well a tattoo.

Ta Moko is a Maori body art practice which shows that the wearer has status within the community. Ta Moko can also tell the story of the wearer's family heritage.

It was not always so.

From the earliest times, tattoos almost always meant trouble. First the Greeks and then the Romans inked the unconsenting backs of prisoners and slaves. The practice continued in Europe throughout the Middle Ages to mark the deviant and the incarcerated.

The indelible cruelty of the prison tattoo can still be seen living in the flesh of those who survived

FOLLOWERS
There are **12,615** followers

BLOG ARCHIVE
□ ▼ 2011 (41)
○▼ March (19)

ABOUT ME
Helen Day

No tattoos before you're thirty. What I'll tell my children…
Sam de Brito
Published by Penguin Australia, 2006

the concentration camps of World War II. There is little that suggests the horror of this genocide more than these numbered tattoos.

For millennia, and with few exceptions, ink on the body signified ownership and brutality. These tattoos were an indication of control, a sign that the bearer had a value that hovered somewhere between property and machine.

When something is imposed without our consent, we tend to develop a strong sense of satire. From at least the 18th century, those who had been marked by the State as 'deviant' began to create their own tattoos.

Convicts were known to mock the King by having the words, 'Property of Mother England' etched into the flesh on their backs. By these means, those who flogged them were reminded that they were vandalizing the property of the Crown.

In the 20th century, those traditions of defiance persisted. In the 1990s, tattoo artists set up shop in every Australian shopping strip. And it was in one of these new body modification boutiques that I and many other young women, dared to 'defile' our femininity. Back then, a handful of use angry young things had symbols of our gender affixed to our own bodies. Tattoos have now become sexy and even adorn the ankle of the British Prime Minister's wife! Personally, I find this profoundly annoying. Here I am stuck not with a real memory of my feminist youth but an indelible kinship to Britain.

The tattoo has been commodified and now performs, more or less, as it originally did; it is fashion's proprietary mark. It's difficult of course to imagine a time when a tattoo marked anyone, man or woman, as a try hard. For a brief moment, however, I did feel the reckless abandon of Carnevale* unfolding on my skin. And now, I look at the symbol of my rebellion and I see an ornament as ordinary as any other cosmetic quirk.

*Carnevale – a Venetian festival at which people wear costumes and masks which conceal their identities.

Examination assessment criteria

The examination will address all the criteria. All student responses will be assessed against each criterion. The extent to which the response is characterised by:

Section C – Analysis of language use (Using language to persuade)

- understanding of the ideas and points of view in the material presented
- analysis of ways in which language and visual features are used to present a point of view and to persuade readers
- control of the mechanics of the English language to support meaning

Chapter 5

Oral responses

Assessment

SAC requirements

In Unit 3 you may be asked to give an oral presentation on a selected text (Outcome 1) or your point of view on a selected media issue (Outcome 3).

Many schools choose their oral to be on a media issue (Outcome 3) and often, it is the first SAC of the year. The time limit may vary but is generally between 5 and 10 minutes. Visuals are not compulsory. You will be asked to submit a written contention and bibliography before delivering your oral. Palm cards may be used.

See Chapter 1 for the VCAA assessment performance descriptors.

End-of-year examination requirements

There is no oral component in Unit 4 or the end-of-year exam.

About oral presentations

The most effective oral presentations:

- engage and connect with their audience throughout entire speech
- state their contention clearly and outline context of issue
- persuade using logical arguments and techniques that appeal to audience
- are delivered competently and with passion and /or enthusiasm
- are prepared, researched thoroughly and satisfy time requirement.

You may adopt a persona for your oral presentation, e.g. an expert talking to young athletes about the dangers of drugs in sport. If you do this, remember to address the audience in character and to be convincing at all times.

DON'T PANIC! To avoid unnecessary stress, follow the C ROAD.

C ROAD to oral presentations

Choose issue, point of view and contention wisely.
Research.
Organise your argument into a logical formal structure.
Add persuasive techniques.
Deliver with confidence.

Choose your issue wisely and form a clear contention

Choose an issue that you are interested in and a presentation type (e.g. speech, oral report or dramatic performance) that you are comfortable with and one that enables you to display a clear POV, contention, logical argument and complex knowledge of an issue.

Note: Your issue must be one *currently* debated in the Australian media, i.e. an issue that has been featured in the Australian media after 30 September of the previous year.

See end of Chapter 2 for a topical issues list.

Always check your issue choice and contention with your English teacher.

Research

Research is very important. You need to use different, reputable sources and to dig deeper than just the first 10 sites listed on a Google search plus Wikipedia. Obviously newspapers and other media online are really useful. Your school may have a password-protected source of information about issues, e.g. echo.

Research your issue thoroughly and take ordered notes. Devise your own A4 version of the following note-taking template to help you.

Issue	
Context What event? When did issue emerge? Issue type and level? Why is it being debated?	

Audience (stereotype them) Associated emotions? Likely appeals?			
Point of view			
Contention			
Source and date	**Main points for**	**Main points against**	**Other**

Hints!

- Use many different sources to gain complex ideas about issue.
- You need at least three to five main points for and one major point to rebut (against).
- Refine your contention if necessary. The more specific your contention, the sharper the focus for your argument.
- Don't forget to acknowledge sources accurately.

Organise your argument logically

Organise your points into a formal presentation structure of introduction, body and conclusion so that you have a cohesive argument and use oral conventions.

No-fail oral presentation structure and techniques

Structure	Components	Techniques
Introduction (You can switch the order of points in your introduction)	**Hook**	• Quote • Statistic • Personal anecdote • Visual image • 'What if?' scenario
	Formal greeting Introduce topic Context and contention Preview 3–5 key points (if wanted)	Use key terms and inclusive language (e.g. 'we', 'us', 'our') Establish tone. Connect with audience.

Body	**Main point 1** Elaboration Evidence Link/connection **Main point 2** Elaboration Evidence Link/connective **Main point 3** Elaboration Evidence Link/connective More main points if necessary **Rebut opposing argument**	*Evidence*: facts, statistics Exaggeration Appeals to audience Rhetorical question(s) – signal change in tone *Signposts*: first, second, next Repetition *Cross reference*: as I said before *Link words*: also, as well, furthermore, moreover, and, unlike. *Rebut links*: however, while some may say that Key terms Visuals
Conclusion	**Call to action** (what they need to do or what needs to happen) Advice Challenge to audience Zinger summary sentence that restates contention Thank audience	*Signpost*: finally, 'I'd like to finish by … ' Key terms Repetition Rhetorical question Visual

Add persuasive language and techniques

Typical persuasive language and techniques for oral presentations are included in the third column of the no-fail oral presentation structure.

- Use a hook to grab your audience's attention at the start, e.g. 'Imagine if …'. 'One in every six teenagers suffers from …'
- Use inclusive language to connect with the audience, e.g. 'we', 'our',' us'.
- Deliver evidence, facts and statistics to support your main points.
- Ask rhetorical questions and use repetition for emphasis.
- Employ exaggeration (hyperbole).
- Tell a brief personal anecdote to connect with the audience.
- Use signposts, connectives and link words so that the speech flows and audience doesn't get lost, e.g. 'first', 'finally', 'in other words', 'however'.
- Use appropriate tones or tonal shift, e.g. from friendly (to connect with audience) to concerned (if warning audience or expert).

Deliver with confidence

Researching and writing a great speech is fine, but you have completed only part of the task. Once you have done that you need to work on your style of delivery, i.e. how you will actually present your speech.

Delivery includes:
- body language (non-verbals)
- palm cards
- visuals
- voice.

Body language

Positive	Maintain eye contact with your audience. Stand straight and tall. Move your hands to convey sizes, shapes, motions and directions. Use a pumped fist, e.g. when saying 'together we can make a difference'. Use one or more fingers to suggest numbers. Point to a visual aid, etc. Make open gestures, e.g. hands widespread.
Negative	Jerky head or arm movements. Swaying, rocking or moving around too much. Scratching or tugging at parts of your body. Keeping hands in pockets. Fiddling with pen, keys, etc. Avoiding eye contact with audience. Folded arms. Slouching.

Palm cards

1 Print or type notes in point form using capital letters.
2 Use headings to organise points.
3 Only two or three points per card.
4 Include instructions such as 'cue visual', 'pause' and 'look up'.
5 Always number your palm cards (in case you drop them).

PALM CARD 1

INTRO PART 1

SHOULD AUST INSTALL MORE CCTV CAMERAS?

3 THINGS CCTV CAMERAS SHOULD DO:

1. REDUCE CRIME
2. INCREASE PUBLIC SAFETY
3. CREATE A SAFE PLACE FOR LEISURE AND PLEASURE

[LOOK UP]

Visuals

It is not a VCAA requirement to use visuals during your oral presentation. A visual can include a videoclip, yourself in a costume, a handout, words on a whiteboard, a prop or a PowerPoint presentation. If you intend using visuals, read the following hints first.

Hints for using visuals

- Ask yourself two questions:
  1. Does the visual enhance (make better) my presentation?
  2. Can I leave out the visuals?
- Do not use visual to merely 'take up time'.
- Make sure that media or YouTube clips are short, relevant and not offensive.
- If handwriting on a whiteboard, make sure it's legible and write it up beforehand.
- If you intend showing something that may offend the audience (e.g. animal deaths, violence, swearing or racist remarks), check first with your teacher..
- Avoid 'death by PowerPoint' where speakers bore their audience by reading every word of a zillion slides.
- Always check that multimedia works *before* your presentation.

Voice

Feature	Advice
Pace	• Don't speed-talk. • Record yourself when you practise. Obtain feedback. • It's better to speak too slowly than too fast.
Volume	• Make sure that your voice can be heard. • Do you need to use a microphone?
Pitch and tone	• Pitch = whether your voice sounds high, squeaky or low. You need to vary your pitch throughout your speech to avoid a boring monotone. • Tone = how you sound about your topic and towards your audience, e.g. friendly, concerned.
Diction Pronunciation	• Pronounce words clearly, e.g. 't' and 'd' at the ends of words. Make sure that you can pronounce any difficult terminology correctly. Avoid mumbling.
Emphasis/stress	• Emphasise or stress key terms that you want to stand out to your audience. Imagine that the word is bold. You might pronounce it more clearly, a little louder or pause before and after the word.
Pause	• Pausing can help stress important points. It's like giving your audience a chance to absorb the point. Sometimes a pause is followed by repetition to further emphasise a point. • Sometimes a pause is used to great effect after a rhetorical question or call to action, e.g. 'Ask yourself. What can I do to help?'

Hints for oral presentations

1 Research and listen and observe effective speakers and famous speeches.
2 Rehearse in front of someone who will provide constructive criticism.
3 Look at the audience while you speak. Do not read the speech.
4 Avoid negative body language. Scratching body parts is a big no-no!
5 Time presentation before SAC and check the pronunciation of difficult words.
6 Don't speed-talk. Use short simple sentences in plain (formal) English.
7 If you make a mistake, take a deep breath and start again.
8 Use numbered palm cards written in point form – this stops you reading.
9 Make sure any multimedia is relevant, easily seen and heard.
10 Always remember to greet and thank audience.

What not to do

1 Speed-talk.
2 Scratch body parts.
3 Avoid eye contact with everyone.
4 Whisper or mumble.
5 Laugh at serious or sad parts.

Oral response checklist

1 Introduction grabs audience's attention. ☐
2 Point of view is identified at start. ☐
3 Points are presented in logical sequence. ☐
4 Signposts have been used. ☐
5 Formal language rules have been followed. ☐
6 Palm cards are written and numbered. ☐
7 Visuals and handouts can be easily read. ☐
8 Prepared answers to at least three questions. ☐
9 Presentation has been rehearsed. ☐
10 Multimedia required is working. ☐

DIY rubric for oral presentation

High-level response	**Medium-level response**	**Low-level response**
Demonstrated understanding of context of issue	Minimal understanding of context of issue	No understanding of context of issue
Clear contention presented	Contention presented but not clearly.	Contention not presented.
Logical complex argument constructed with main points	Some complex argument constructed with main points	Little or no complex argument constructed with main points
Appropriate tone(s) used in relation to issue.	Appropriate tone(s) used in relation to issue for some part of presentation.	Inappropriate tone(s) used in relation to issue.
Sufficient researched evidence presented to support points, e.g. facts, statistics, experts, appeals, visuals (optional)	Some researched evidence presented to support points e.g. facts, statistics, experts, appeals, visuals (optional)	Insufficient researched evidence presented to support points e.g. facts, statistics, experts, appeals, visuals (optional)

Oral language and presentation conventions used, e.g. greeting; signposts and connectives; clear intro, body, conclusion structure: call to action: inclusive language: rhetorical questions; repetition	Some oral language and presentation conventions used, e.g. greeting; signposts and connectives; clear intro, body, conclusion structure: call to action; inclusive language: rhetorical questions; repetition	Little or no oral language and presentation conventions used, e.g greeting; signposts and connectives; clear intro, body, conclusion structure: call to action: inclusive language: rhetorical questions; repetition
Clear connection/ engagement with audience demonstrated	Some connection/ engagement with audience demonstrated	No connection/ engagement with audience demonstrated
Appropriate body language including gesture and eye contact	Appropriate body language but little eye contact	Inappropriate body language including gesture and little or no eye contact
Appropriate pace and volume	Inconsistent volume and pace	Inappropriate volume and/or pace

Practice activities

1 Introductions

Read and compare the introductions of the following four oral presentations on CCTV cameras, freedom of speech and banning live animal exports.

Note: There are two speech transcripts on banning live animal exports. The second speech is written by an EAL student.

Identify the:

(a) issue
(b) context
(c) contention
(d) techniques used.

2 Transcript analysis

(a) Spend 15–20 minutes reading the transcript for CCTV cameras.
(b) Construct a 'no-fail OP structure and techniques' chart and identify as many structure features, main points and persuasive techniques as you can from the speech
(c) Do the same for the freedom of speech transcript.

3 Comparison of speeches

(a) Examine both speeches on banning live animal exports and identify as many structure features, main points and persuasive techniques as you can from the speech.
(b) Comment on what you think the likely impact would be on the audience.
(c) Compare the speeches. Which do think is more effective? Why?

4 Famous speeches

Research and view, listen to or read famous speeches, e.g. Paul Keating's speech at Redfern, Barack Obama's inaugural speech as US President and Steve Jobs's Stanford address. Google 'TED Talks'.

5 DIY speech audit

Video your practice oral response and analyse it objectively, concentrating on your delivery. Use the DIY oral presentation rubric.

Sample speech transcript 1

CCTV cameras

Good morning, everyone. The topic that I'm doing is, 'Should Australia install more CCTV cameras?'

There are three things that a CCTV camera should strive to do:

1 Reduce crime.

2 Improve public safety.

3 Create a safe place for the leisure and pleasure of citizens and tourists.

As we all know, the issue of whether Australia should or should not install more CCTV cameras has arisen due to the recent murder of Jill Meagher, whose abductor was caught on camera.

I am one of the many people who believe that there is a huge exaggeration of the usefulness of these cameras, and that we as a country do *not* need to install any more.

Just before I go into further detail about my point of view on this issue, I want to tell you a little story that I discovered while watching a documentary a while ago.

One exotic fish was going missing from an aquarium every night. The attendant was suspected but denied it. CCTV cameras were installed. It was discovered that an octopus from a nearby tank was sneaking out and eating one fish every night.

Yes, that is an interesting story, but I know that you are probably wondering what the actual relevance of it is, and maybe some of you are thinking that it contradicts my view on CCTV cameras. But what I really wanted to tell you is that this tiny little octopus case is only an extremely small-scale problem. While octopuses are very intelligent creatures, they are not smart enough to actually know that the security camera was there. Therefore, how were they meant to realise they were going to be watched and ultimately caught?

My point here is that people who are going to commit a crime don't just jump straight in there and do it – they think, they prepare, they plan and they are strategic. And, in saying that, I mean that they will cover their faces, assume a disguise, tactically block out camera lenses while also avoiding as many cameras as possible. Installing more security cameras won't prevent people from committing crimes – it will simply encourage them to slyly slip under the radar.

It has been claimed that security cameras have little if no effect on reducing crime. Well, it's because the locations of security cameras are so easily advertised for anyone to see.

Sure, this is because shop owners and workplaces want to seem intimidating, but unknowingly this is actually makes it easier for people to spot the cameras, to sneak through, avoid being detected and commit easily their crime. And like I said before, increasing the amount of cameras is just simply encouraging people to become better at their crimes and will most definitely not reduce the rate of crime occurring.

According to certain studies, only 4% of CCTV cameras have actually prevented crimes. Another study in London showed that only one crime was solved for every 1000 cameras that were installed. Imagine that 1000 people from our senior school were randomly abducted and murdered, and only [add name from audience]'s abductor was caught on camera, so out of 1000 different murders, [name from audience]'s was the only one that was solved. This just puts it in perspective for us all just how little security cameras actually do.

David Vile, the vice chair of the Australian Privacy foundation stated, 'You can still be murdered, raped, bashed, robbed or harassed and walking in front of the CCTV camera doesn't necessarily protect you from that.'

Every single day, horrible things such as murder and rape occur, and only a few of these cases are actually captured on a camera. And what David Vile is trying to say, even though the camera might, I'm emphasising *might*, capture the harasser or murderer, it's not like the camera can actually do anything about it. So even though the camera catches the person who murdered ______, it's not like the camera is able to stop that person from pulling the trigger and murdering ______.

The majority of these horrible murder and harassment cases are never solved, never publicised, and as a country we don't get to hear anything about it as we prefer to ignore these things and delude ourselves into believing that we live in a safe, secure and protected environment. The cameras themselves actually can't help prevent the crime, they can't help the victim, so what's the point in increasing them?

Yet another negative aspect of CCTV cameras is that they cost so much to install and maintain. I'm sure that most of you have heard of the Louvre in Paris. If you haven't, all you need to know is that it's an incredibly famous museum. Being so worldly renowned the Louvre most definitely contains a huge amount of CCTV cameras. But what you might not know is that not all these CCTV cameras actually work – they're just for show. Sure, the ones that are focused on high-valued paintings such as the *Mona Lisa* or *Madonna of the Rocks* definitely are functioning and recording, but there are quite a few cameras focused on low-profile paintings or artworks that don't actually work. And this is because it is simply too expensive to pay for functioning cameras around the whole museum.

As of 2012, there have been 53 CCTV cameras installed in Victoria, specifically our Melbourne CBD, and these cost roughly half a million dollars to run annually. Just think about that, only 53 cameras, roughly this size, costing half a million dollars. And that's just in Victoria, oh no sorry … just in the Melbourne CBD! Should we seriously waste all our hard-earned money on installing additional CCTV cameras that aren't even guaranteed to protect our society? NO, I don't think so.

Another point to consider is that with increasing amounts of live CCTV, it is impossible for all the footage to be monitored. In Western Australia, police claim that they watch 596 cameras across the state, and by later this year, there will be over 5000 additional cameras to watch, a physically impossible task, and huge waste of money. There is no point in installing those extra 5000 CCTV cameras if they aren't even going to be watched.

Finally, I just want to share with you that one of the most disturbing things about CCTV cameras is that they can be easily used and manipulated to invade people's privacy.

The amount of footage these days that is violated for the personal benefit of the viewers is incredibly disturbing and quite seriously disgusting and for this reason, more cameras should definitely not be installed. For example:

- Bathrooms in Chadstone – walk daily through the strip of shops to the bus
- Trying on clothes in Myer – at any given point in any given time.

If we want to reduce crime, improve public safety and create a safe place for the leisure and pleasure of citizens and tourists, then we need better alternatives to costly CCTV cameras. Alternatives that work. Let's put more police on the streets. Let's increase lighting in dark streets. Let's encourage citizens to report any suspicious activity.

I believe Australia should *not* install additional security cameras as it is a huge violation of our privacy and an extreme waste of money and they don't even prevent crime from occurring.

Thank you.

(1214 words)

Sample speech transcript 2

Freedom of speech

'If you want total security, go to prison. There you're fed, clothed, given medical care and so on. The only thing lacking ... is freedom.' This was the view that Eisenhower adopted about liberties. The looming issue associated to the balance in society, whether it is acceptable to sacrifice an individual's civil liberties in the interest of national and personal security. As humans we have the right to feel safe and protected, but this doesn't mean the government has the right to invade our personal freedoms. Freedom is the power to determine our action without restraint from a higher power. What the government proposes to do with certain new laws isn't security; it's taking away our personal freedoms as a citizen. If we allow the government to rule over us with an inescapable power we will find ourselves being watched at every corner, false security and racial tension created in our airports and the illusion of freedom of speech.

In America they call themselves the land of the free, however, what is so free about being watched at every street corner? In the UK 20,000 euro has been spent on CCTV cameras for the city yet these have only assisted in solving one crime. One crime! Not only is this a waste of money but a waste of time for the police. Behind every CCTV camera there are five officers that could be patrolling our streets. The police force of London admitted that for every 1000 cameras in London, less than one crime is solved per year. Britain has one per cent of the world's population but has bought the most CCTV cameras. At this rate that means that there is 1 for every 14 people, and only one crime is being solved a year. This has led to a mass expense, an intrusion of privacy and little prevention of crime, if any. What kind of freedom is that?

After 9/11 airport security went through the roof with new laws and regulations. And this has led to a massive outbreak of discrimination within society. Michel Kinsey wrote an article on the 'discrimination we are afraid to be against' and highlighted the idea that the people working in the security for airports have a rational sense of who is a threat to other people. Kinsey simply says 'An Arab-looking man heading towards a plane is statistically more likely to be a terrorist ...' Come on, we have fought for years against discrimination and still we are all so race orientated. Who are we to say that because of your skin colour you can't enjoy the same freedoms as others. This is an invasion of people's rights to feel safe within their own skin. Because of different beliefs, race and religion. The accusation that Kinsey made is not only horrific but vulgar and distasteful towards many individuals.

Freedom of speech, the right to know the truth is part of having civil liberties. In China the government has blocked off many Internet sites to the population and has limited media broadcasting so that the government can cover up their wrongs. The Chinese government has taken away the people's right to know the truth, thus violating the civil liberties of these people. Wikileaks is an anonymous site which allows people to give secure tips to journalists who provide our society with the truth. The government is insecure regarding their wrongdoings and firmly argues that complete truth or transparency is undesirable when dealing with the 'frenzied masses'. Due to this many governments have been actively seeking an end to Wikileaks. Surely this is doing just what the government of China has done to its people? Our government is trying to choose for us. That is not security, it is taking away a person's right to know information and their freedom to speak. I refuse to be held captive within some kind of government manufactured society, freedom should be the foremost desire for the individual.

Simone Weil, 20th century French philosopher, manufactures an ideal world or utopia while keeping the intellect, soul and body sustained and nourished. Weil contends the soul has 14 vital needs and to attain balance within our society we must follow the soul's needs. She states that 'liberty, taking the word in its concrete sense, consists in its ability to choose.' While security likens a state of permanent fear to 'a semi-paralysed [state] of the soul', used to enslave or infect people. Basically Weil illustrates a world where we as humans have the ability to choose, but only to the extent that she chooses. Thus suggesting that one's 'rights' do not stem from the individual to which they belong, but from another; wherein they exist as an obligation. The biggest issue with Weil's utopia is that it is highly idealistic and this insular model could not exist within society today. Fundamentally, this society exists absent of crime and even fear. While this seems ideal it is clear that the citizens cannot understand the depths of their own indoctrination, hence, freedom is completely sacrificed.

It's independence, the licence to do what we want, freedom to choose for ourselves. That's the society that I want to live in, and I think it's the one you want to live in too. Give me freedom and unchain me from the burden of society, from their racial differences, from Big Brother's eyes, from my government's constant need to pretend I'm allowed to speak my mind. I don't want your utopia that latches onto my soul. Patrick Henry once declared that 'Is life so dear, or peace so sweet, as to be purchased at the price of chains or slavery? Forbid it, Almighty God! I know not what course others may take but as for me; give me liberty or give me death!'

Thank you

Sample speech transcript 3

Australia should ban live animal exports

Picture this:

You are tied by a rope around your neck.
A person behind you is jabbing you with a sharp stick to keep you moving.
You try to kick it away again and again until with one last kick you slip on the blood-soaked floor and come crashing down, snapping your leg in half. Pain shoots through your body.
You try, but you can't get up. You try again and come crashing down.
Becoming impatient, the men break your arm. Still you can't move, yet they poke your eyes and pull at your ears.
You try to get up, anything to stop the torture, but you come crashing down, smashing your skull on the hard, cold concrete floor.

You cry as they pour water up your nostrils to stop you breathing. You are kicked, nine times in total, until finally your throat is slit and you bleed to death. You scream as you feel your warm blood escaping your body.

This is a true story. It happened to an Australian cow transported to Indonesia, but this is not an isolated case.

Today I will argue that the live animal export trade *must* be banned in Australia. It is time **we** stand up for our livestock and put an end to this senseless torture once and for all.

The primary reasons for this are numerous: Australia is unable to ensure humane slaughtering practices will be followed overseas; and many animals suffer and die in transit. A system of regulations that allow exporters to detect animal abuse is not enough; and finally, despite the supposed economic impacts of ending livestock exports, the reality is these are far less significant than suggested.

How can Australia police the way another nation treats our livestock? If our livestock are in other nations, there is nothing we, as Australians, can do. So why would livestock exporters and the Australian government believe they can ensure humane slaughtering practices overseas? We can claim to be humane within our own country all we want, but that means nothing if we deliberately allow others to torture. *There is no moral difference* between allowing someone to do things we consider inhumane and doing them ourselves. The blood is on our hands.

Most of our exported livestock go to the Middle Eastern countries with dominant Islamic cultures – Islam requires cattle to be slaughtered according to Halal standards, that is, slitting the animal's throat with a blade and hanging it up to be drained of its blood while it is still alive. The pain suffered by the animal is inconceivable. There is no stunning involved. The animal is completely conscious. This practice is widespread throughout the Muslim world. In Egypt, cows have the tendons in their legs cut and have a blade forced into their eyes, disabling them before they're slaughtered. The only way to stop the suffering of *our Australian* livestock for good is to ban live animal exports. The facilities exist in Australia for cows to be slaughtered with adherence to Halal standards as certified by Australian-based Islamic agencies, thus rendering the whole process of exporting live cattle completely pointless.

Over the last 30 years some 2.5 million Australian animals have died merely during transit to other countries – it would seem these ones are the lucky ones. The conditions on such ships are unacceptable. About one ship inspected by vet technician Deb Clarke, she stated: 'No one had checked the air-conditioning in the calf unit – and it was over 50 degrees heat – and there were dead and dying animals everywhere, and I was just absolutely heartbroken. Animals were too weak to even stand; they were lying in hot sand. They were frying, literally cooking, and at temperatures of 50-plus degrees; they were frying from the inside out. It was shocking'. These conditions are unacceptable; what makes it worse is that they are being loaded in Australian ports – truly, we are responsible.

If the live export trade were to be stopped and banned, the economic impact would be negligible. On average, the live export trade for sheep and cattle is roughly $789 million dollars per year. This may seem a lot; however, in the context of the $1.5 trillion Australian economy the amount lost would be a relatively insignificant 0.05% of nominal GDP. Regardless, due to the live export industry losing confidence since the temporary ban to Indonesia, current property prices are down and banks are unwilling to give out loans. This means that a phasing out of livestock exports will bring back confidence as producers will be able to export frozen carcasses, providing a more promising future for the industry. Frozen meat is in demand, and producers are able to make shipments more efficiently. In 2005 the total value of processed meat exports was over $5.9 billion compared to around $700 million for live exports. Regulation does not kill economies – uncertainty does. Uncertainty over the future of live exports means that exporters are not finding ways to export their product in a more humane fashion, but are merely playing the waiting game – by outlawing live exports we can provide a clear path for these industries to move forward.

Australia's system of regulations designed to detect and stop animal abuse is flawed. In Karachi, Pakistan last year 21 000 *Australian* sheep were brutally and savagely buried alive, some had their throats cut, while others had their necks snapped by men using only their bare hands. Why? Because they were said to have been diseased, which has since been proven to have been incorrect. These animals suffered horrible deaths for no reason and Australia could do nothing to prevent it. The Australian-standard slaughter houses in Indonesia and Pakistan still slaughter animals in ways that would sicken any reasonable person. Australia's system of livestock regulations does not work. I quote Labor MP Kelvin Thompson: 'If the system of regulation works, it works in the sense that an ambulance at the bottom of the cliff works.' Again we must think hard and decide – is there a difference between knowingly allowing others to continue these actions and carrying them out ourselves? I think not.

In conclusion: every hour, 50 Australian cows are being slaughtered overseas. These cows will survive horrible conditions in transit only to be brutally tortured and slaughtered. *Let's take a stand together* to remove the live export trade from Australia.

Thank you

Sample speech transcript 4 by an EAL student

We should ban live animal testing

Science has blood on its hands. [Lessen impact] The blood of foetuses, killed so that we can study their stem cells. The blood of innocent civilians in Hiroshima and Nagasaki, killed not because the war required it, but because we wanted an opportunity to test our science. The blood of powerless monkeys, mice, and even dogs and cats, sacrificed so we can test products we don't even need.

We may think of scientific experiment as something done in the past, or in other countries that aren't as advanced as ours, but it is done today, in a civilised society like Australia. In a report released December last year by the Victorian government that was picked up by *The Age*, it was revealed that extensive animal testing is still going on in Victoria – with almost half a million lab animals dying in 2011 alone. That figure does not include almost 2 million poultry and fish, but it does include domestic dogs, domestic cats, horses and seals.

We continue to perform scientific tests on animals, tests that cause their death, even in an age and in a country where we say we believe in animal rights.
These unnecessary and unreliable tests should not be done.

Firstly, due to the inherent difference between human and other species, animal testing does not precisely tell us how a substance will affect the human body.
There are drugs that would not see the light of the day if they were tested on animals. Penicillin, for instance, is lethal to pigs and causes severe birth defects in rats. Yet it is, as our experience could easily tell, a mighty medicine for us.
The other side of this is that most drugs fail in human clinical trials because until that point they have relied on animal testing to predict the behaviour of the drug on humans. In an open letter a group of British scientists sent to their prime minister, it was pointed out that 90% of drug trials FAIL because animal reactions aren't the same as human reactions. A question, therefore, must be asked: if animal testing is only 10% accurate, why are we still using it? We are trading lives for 10% accuracy.

Secondly, the majority of our current animal experiments are unnecessary or have alternatives. Academics and scientists who work in the area themselves don't see the need for continued animal testing. Professor Peter Taylor, director of the Victorian Life Sciences computation initiative at the University of Melbourne, for example, is confident that we could do all the testing 'in silica' – in other words, in a computer environment. In this era of computer science, supercomputers could be a substitution that is easy, cheap, harmless, and efficient. Another instance of the sheer pointlessness of animal testing is the whaling for research. The Japanese officially explain their purpose of whaling as research for whale management. In other words, they need to kill whales to learn how to manage living whales – but, unfortunately, this type of unnecessary animal experiments could not eliminate the management problem, [heavy satire] unless they killed all whales. [good use of humour]

It is important to acknowledge that there is another side to this argument as well, though. [need a smoother transition] It is recognised that animal testing is regulated to try to manage the harm it causes. Since the proclamation of the Animal Welfare Act 1999, we have had a detailed regulation of how animals should be treated in testings. Their death or suffering is confined to situations offering 'significant advancement' or 'educational purposes'. There are two problems with this regulation, however. The first is the vague wording of the criteria – what advancement is 'significant', how likely does it need to be, and would ANY educational purpose qualify? The second problem is the enforcer of these rules. As Cherie Wilson, a former ethics committee member at the Department of Primary Industries highlighted, the committee is merely a 'rubber stamp'. Their job, apart from ensuring that no lost pets end up as subjects of experiments, is to approve experiments. The ridiculousness of this rubber stamp approval is exemplified by an experiment that was part of the Northern Affairs project. It can be outlined as follows: The Aim: to determine whether or not polar bears can swim in crude oil. The Method: let a polar bear swim in a tank of oil. The Observation: The bear swam, got out, licked its fur clean, and died due to ingestion of oil. The Conclusion: polar bears cannot swim in oil. [Sarcasm] Thanks to the Department of Primary Industries, our pet cats or dogs do not have to swim in oil.

The issue of animal testing within science is important, but on a larger scale, this smaller issue leads us to the even bigger ethical question: What sacrifices can we morally support in the short term or on a small scale, in order to possibly make some advances? [Pause] In the aforementioned report from December last year, it is mentioned that the number of lab animal deaths has tripled every year since 2010. If this trend were continuous, in less than 20 years the animal population of Victoria could be wiped out. Although this scenario seems extreme, it does show us that sacrifice and loss will be the price of new technology.

Because we do not get scientific advancement for free, there is always a cost. We see, in the December report, the matter that we ignore, the tragedy that we caused: death of millions. And our blind belief that scientists always know which sacrifices are worth making should be changed. There must be a line drawn, beyond which we say an absolute no to the testings, regardless of whether science may find a possible future benefit from them.

This line could be that an animal is not to be killed in testings unless a specific human's life will nearly certainly be saved. In other words, on a slightly bigger scale, this approach could be thought of as protecting what we already have first, before endangering it for something potential in the future.

The consequences of not having and enforcing such a line are clear. Firstly, past experience tells us that science can end up with bloodied hands. Human lives have been the cost of science even nowadays. This January, the *Sydney Morning Herald* reported the death of Indian bricklayer Azghar Khan, due to a trial vitamin drug from an Australian company. You see, the blood is on the hands of Australians, and it is on them today – not just in WWII. Secondly, without drawing this line to tell science what it cannot do, the vulnerable will not be well-protected. It seems that we never question science. As long as [emphasise] scientists are involved, we trust them to do the [emphasise] right thing. Yet, do they? Will they ever suggest to us that the millions spent on weapon development, on researching killing, could be spent on health care? Will they even think about the homeless, the disabled, those in need, when using our hard earned money to buy another [sarcasm] polar bear? In addition to animals, who do not have a choice, there are many costs and victims of research – many of them unrecognised or thought of as necessary sacrifices. Don't we owe them a responsibility to speak on their behalf, though?

To conclude, the line between what is ethical and what is not is difficult to draw; if it was not, this would not be an issue. There is no easy test for when testing is ethically acceptable. But, because it is a difficult question, a lot of people ignore it and leave it to the scientists to decide. Though the line cannot be determined, its approximate location at the moment is apparent: on the side of short term sacrifice, in exchange for potential future benefit. In other words, we should focus on protecting and take less risk. Even it means we do not get all the advancement we might otherwise gain, we should prioritise social responsibility to the people and things *here and now*, who are vulnerable in the present moment, lest we want the hands of science to be forever bloodied.

Bibliography:
www.animalsaustralia.org/take_action/live-export
www.liveexport-indefensible.com
www.echoeducation.com.au/schools/doca2012/liveexports2012/argumentspro.php
http://en.wikipedia.org/wiki/Live_export
www.daff.gov.au/animal-plant-health/welfare/export-trade/benefits
http://theconversation.edu.au/the-live-export-of-animals-will-always-be-a-bloody-business-10547
www.abc.net.au/4corners/content/2011/s3230934.htm

Topic:
We should ban live animal exports.

Purpose:
To persuade the audience to agree that we should ban the trade.

Audience:
Addressing Year 12 students.

Chapter 6

How to write a point-of-view text

About point-of-view texts

You may have to write a point-of-view text on a selected issue as part of your SAC for Outcome 3 in Unit 3. It may be for an oral presentation (see Chapter 5) or a written text such as an essay, editorial or article.

See Chapter 1 for assessment criteria and performance descriptors.

Writing a point-of-view text means writing using a persuasive style and creating an argumentative text. You can write as yourself, a Year 12 student, or you may choose to write assuming a persona, e.g. a columnist in a newspaper or an expert giving a speech. There are many different forms you can use to write a point-of-view text and steps you can follow to write an engaging and effective point-of-view text.

Forms suited to point-of-view texts include:

- a transcript for a speech to be given at a student or community forum
- a formal letter to the editor of a newspaper
- an editorial or feature article for a newspaper for the school or wider community
- a personal column
- assuming the writing style of a regular columnist
- an essay for an anthology for the school and wider community.

Six steps to writing a point-of-view text

1 Choose your issue, form, contention and audience wisely 2 Research the issue and your chosen form 3 Organise your argument logically 4 Add persuasive language and techniques 5 Write 6 Review and edit

1 Choose your issue, form, contention and audience wisely

(a) Choose an issue that you are interested in. You need to display a clear POV, contention, logical argument and complex knowledge of an issue.

- Your issue must be one *currently* debated in the Australian media, i.e. an issue that has been featured in the Australian media after 30 September of the previous year.
- See end of Chapter 2 for a topical issues list.
- Always check your issue choice with your English teacher.

(b) Choose to write using a form that shows your strengths.
(c) Write a clear contention and check with your English teacher.
(d) Own your form. Research, know and use conventions.
(e) Always choose an audience that is VCE or above, in order to be able to use complex ideas and language.

- Stereotype your audience so that you know what persuasive strategies will work best to convince them of your point of view.
- See Chapter 2 for information on how to stereotype the audience.

2 Research the issue and your chosen form

(a) Research the issue thoroughly and take ordered notes. Devise your own A4 version of the note-taking template in Chapter 5 to help you.

Hints!

- Use many different sources to gain complex ideas about issue.
- You need three to five main points for and one major point to rebut (against).
- Refine your contention if necessary. The more specific your contention, the sharper the focus for your argument.
- Don't forget to acknowledge sources accurately.

(b) Research your chosen form. If you choose to write a personal column, your piece must look and read like a personal column.
Find out the following:

- Does it have a headline, byline and email address at bottom?
- What persuasive strategies are used, e.g. emotive language?
- Where is contention stated?
- What is the general structure?
- How would you describe the language style?
- What is the tone and/or tonal shift?

3 Organise your argument logically

Organise your points for and against into a logical structure that suits your chosen form. Use topic sentences at the start of your body paragraphs.

Point-of-view text structure and techniques

Form	General structure	Techniques
Title/headline Introduction (*You can switch the order of points in your introduction)	Hook	• Quote • Statistic • Personal anecdote • Visual image • 'What if?' scenario
Byline	*Introduce topic Context and contention Preview 3–5 key points (if wanted)	Use key terms and inclusive language. Establish tone.
Body	Main point 1 Elaboration Evidence Link/connective	Language style that suits readers, e.g. emotive, personal, logical *Evidence*: facts, statistics, expert Appeals to audience *Link words*: also, furthermore, moreover, and, unlike, however Other techniques that suit form and audience. Key terms
	Main point 2 Elaboration Evidence Link/connective	
	Main point 3 Elaboration Evidence Link/connective	
	More main points if necessary	
	Rebut opposing argument	
Conclusion of 1 or 2 sentences Email address	Call to action/advice Challenge to audience Zinger summary sentence that restates contention	Key terms Repetition Rhetorical question

4 Add persuasive language and techniques

Typical persuasive language and techniques for point-of-view text include:

- a headline
- a hook to grab your audience's attention at the start
- a language style that suits your form, e.g. personal and reflective for personal column
- inclusive and exclusive language
- evidence including facts and statistics to support the main points
- rhetorical questions and repetition to emphasise points
- personal anecdotes

- connectives and link words so that speech flows and the audience doesn't get lost, e.g. 'furthermore', 'however'.
- appropriate tone or tonal shift, e.g. from friendly (to connect with the audience) to concerned (if warning the audience) or friendly to authoritative (if assuming a persona of expert).

5 Write

Use a clear structure and aim for five to seven paragraphs (80–1200 words). Read and follow 'Five ways to improve your writing' below.

Five ways to improve your writing

Two different writers could be given the same topic and one text could be fascinating to read while the other may put you in a coma. What makes some texts interesting and others dead boring? No matter what style you write in, to make your text interesting you need to think about what texts grab your attention and keep it.

1 Complexity	• A clear contention (spine) • At least three key points/arguments (bones) • Evidence and persuasive technique (flesh) • Key terms • 800–1200 words • Language must suit chosen audience and form.
2 Convincing	• Own your form. Be an expert in your chosen form. • Know the conventions of your chosen form, e.g. greeting, personal example, inclusive language, rhetorical questions, and repetition in speeches. • Use any special visual features, e.g. headline, journalist's byline at start of article, or email address at bottom of an article. • Research – convincing voice. • Write what you know. • Project a strong voice.
3 Hook reader from the start	• Statistics, quotes, personal anecdotes, strong visuals or images • Active voice • Present tense
4 Logical and clear structure	• Introduction–body–conclusion • Ideas and evidence linked • Evidence and persuasive techniques woven into sentences to support points • Connective (link words)

	• Use topic sentences at start of each body paragraph.
5 Proofread and edited	• Key terms used and spelt correctly • Use paragraphs and capital letters.

6 Review and edit

Edited work is easier to read and earns you more marks. Use the following checklist and PETs from chapter 4 to help you edit your work.

Point-of-view text checklist

1 Conventions of form have been followed. □
2 Point of view on the issue is clearly stated. □
3 Language suits chosen audience, form and context. □
4 Tone(s) suit chosen form. □
5 Argument is supported by factual evidence. □
6 Structure is logical, uses connectives and link words. □
7 Effective persuasive techniques and language are used. □
8 The main opposing argument is rebutted. □
9 The piece grabs readers' attention from the start. □
10 Accurate spelling, grammar and punctuation are used. □

Chapter 7

End-of-year examination advice

About the end-of-year examination

The end-of-year English exam is:

- a common assessment task worth 50% of your study score
- usually the first exam
- three hours in length with 15 minutes reading time
- set by external panel
- marked externally, not by your English teachers
- sat by all English students, although EAL students do a modified version
- composed of three sections (weighted equally for mainstream students).

Section	Mainstream	EAL
Section A	One extended analytical/ expository text response to texts from List 1.	One extended analytical/ expository text response to texts from List 1.
Section B	One extended piece (expository, persuasive, imaginative) using ideas from the selected context and direct reference to at least one text for context	One extended piece (expository, persuasive, imaginative) using ideas from the selected context and direct reference to at least one text for context
Section C	One extended analysis of written language and visual features in unseen text(s).	Part 1 Note-form summary. Part 2 Analysis of how written language and visual features persuade readers about three main points in summary.

[VCAA Study Design 2007–2015]

Key points about language analysis from 2013 assessor's report

- Strong language skills (including correct spelling and grammar) are expected and necessary for success.
- It is recommended that students organise their time so that enough time is left to proofread their work.
- While handwriting is not assessed, it must be legible.
- Pay careful attention to the 'Background Information', which should ensure a good understanding of the context of the piece presented.
- Analyse different points of argument. Don't focus on just one point.
- Explore *how* language is being used to persuade rather than technique identification.
- Focus on the tone – why is it being used and how does it change throughout a piece? Avoid simply including words from a generalised list of tone words. Think about *how* text sounds.
- Incorporate visuals into analysis.
- Use as much of the provided material as possible.
- Analyse visuals instead of simply describing them.
- Descriptions such as 'appealing to bandwagon jumping', 'appeal to parents' or 'appeal to authority' are generalised comments and, without more detailed exploration, add little to the piece.
- Read the piece holistically and analyse its whole intention.
- Identify contrasts used as a persuasive devices e.g. alternative proposals regarded as 'fenced and concreted' or 'yet another carpark'.

Key points about language analysis from 2013 EAL assessor's report

Part 1 note form

- Some students didn't grasp the historical and wider references.
- Note-form responses mostly demonstrated an awareness of the key reasons for the speaker's contention but were not always as clear on the contention.
- Choosing the form of 'yes/no' or 'positive/negative' presents main ideas satisfactorily but does not always allow inclusion of the overall message.

Part 2

- Some students struggled to accurately describe tone and included long lists of adjectives describing many different and extreme tones.

- Most students recognised that the audience had a mixed age range but may not have realised that audience was made up of enthusiastic readers.
- Responses need to be constructed around ideas, not persuasive techniques.
- The photograph was generally understood, but the cartoon was generally misunderstood.

What high-range responses showed

- A clear understanding of context and writer's point of view.
- A focus on analysis of the language, not argument.
- An explanation of how the council as well as the residents might react.
- Clear explanation linking visuals to the writer's point of view and exploring the intended effect of visuals.

The use of 'readers' instead of 'audience' or 'listeners' is a common error.

Advice – what students should do

- Examine and analyse existing model answers.
- Practise note-form responses with shorter, one-sided pieces, e.g. letters to the editor.
- Improve their skills in presenting notes in a variety of ways.
- Write about how language persuades and not just label persuasive language.
- Read the background information carefully.
- Relate language persuasion to a specific audience.
- Introductions should be limited to showing an awareness of the audience, context and overall contention of the piece.
- The topic sentence of each following paragraph should identify the point of the argument on which the language analysis will focus.

Exam preparation

Most students stress about exams. The best way to reduce exam stress is to *be prepared*! You should aim to be so prepared that you view the exam as a chance to show off your knowledge and skills. Instead of wasting time and energy stressing about how much revision you have to do, use the following checklist.

Exam preparation checklist

1 Design a study revision timetable that includes 'chill time'. □
2 Maintain a normal routine of sleep, exercise and healthy eating. □
3 Devise a plan of attack for the exam. □
4 Know the assessment criteria and the assessor's report in this chapter. □
5 Practise writing analyses under timed conditions. □

6 Know different persuasive forms and weave structures. □
7 Practise analysing visual language and features. □
8 Revise persuasive language, techniques, appeals. □
9 Know key terms, analysis verbs and connectives (link words). □
10 Have your language analysis writing weapons prepared. □

Time limits

You will complete your SACs under timed conditions, but these are often longer than the time you will have during the end-of-year exam. You need to practise writing under the pressure of time limits before you sit the exam. Do not miss sitting any practice exams.

You can also practise by yourself at home by using past exam papers or topics given by your teacher and timing yourself. Discipline yourself to follow time limits and conditions closely to ensure the best possible practice. Leaving after half an hour to watch your favourite TV show is *not* a good idea.

As well as preparing you for the exam, practising under imposed time limits will help you identify your needs and writing habits. Knowing these can help you devise a plan of attack for the exam that suits you.

Plan of attack

You have three separate sections to complete in the exam, each worth the same amount of marks (mainstream). You need to decide your plan of attack – how long you will spend planning and writing on each section – before the exam.

You must discipline yourself to stick to your plan of attack, no matter what happens. Don't make the mistake of spending too long on one section and then not leaving yourself enough time to complete another section.

Remember the following when deciding your plan of attack:

- There's no such thing as free time in an English exam.
- Make the most of your reading time in the exam.
- Examiners do not assess plans.
- Consider the weighting of each section.

Plan of attack 1

Reading time 15 mins	3 mins to decide topic in Section A and read the Context topic in Section B 12 mins to read through the background information and unseen texts in language analysis. Decide which analysis structure to use.
Section C 65 mins	5 mins to mark up texts 60 mins to write language analysis and edit
Section A 57 mins	2 mins to jot down text quotes and plan essay 55 mins to write text response essay and edit
Section B 58 mins	3 mins to write message, main points, quotes, etc. 55 mins to write context piece and edit
Any leftover time	Proofread and edit more

Plan of attack 2

Reading time	3 mins to decide topic in Section A and read the Context topic in Section B 12 mins to read through the background information and unseen texts in language analysis. Decide which analysis structure to use.
Section A 57 mins	2 mins to jot down text quotes and plan essay 55 mins to write text response essay and edit
Section C 65 mins	5 mins to mark up texts 60 mins to write language analysis and edit
Section B 58 mins	3 mins to write message, main points, quotes etc. 55 mins to write context piece and edit
Any leftover time	Proofread and edit more

Language analysis weapons

- Blue or black pens that don't bleed all over the page (no pencil).
- Highlighters of three different colours.
- Dictionary (decent and recent. Not one with pictures)
- Marking code of your own.
- Plan of attack.
- A clear, calm, cool head.
- Writer's stretches so your hand doesn't ache.
- Watch, so you can adhere to time limits (mobile phones are *not* permitted)
- Handwriting plan if your handwriting is difficult to read.

In the exam

When seated, you will receive a task book, a script book and some extra sheets of paper. You indicate your choice of text and topic in Sections A and B by shading a checkbox. You may take in with you an English and/or bilingual dictionary. These dictionaries will be checked by one of the exam supervisors.

The task book is divided into sections with specific instructions for each section. For Section B you will need to nominate your main text. The assessment criteria for the exam is also written in the task book.

Access VCAA website to see a sample of this task book.

Hints for exam language analysis

1 Once in exam. Take three deep breaths. Don't panic. Believe in yourself.
2 Lay out your pencils, watch, highlighters and dictionary.
3 Stick to your plan of attack and the time limits for each section.
4 Carefully read the background information and texts during reading time.
5 Decide which analysis structure you will use: mini, semi or total weave.
6 Mark up persuasive texts. Identify context, issue, contention and arguments.
7 Stereotype the audience in your head and think about how they would react.
8 Identify tone, tonal shifts and overall language style if you can.
9 Remember COAST and quote fest.
10 Use body paragraphs with topic sentences and what?, how?, what likely audience impact?
11 Make sure your handwriting is legible. Leave lines between paragraphs.
12 Proofread and edit your work, particularly introduction.

Language analysis checklist

1 COAST is used in first paragraph. ☐
2 Relevant features of form are discussed. ☐
3 Tones and tonal shifts of texts are analysed. ☐
4 Body paragraphs have topic sentences = subject matter + tone. ☐
5 Lots of small quotes are used to support points. ☐
6 Arguments and argument structure are analysed. ☐
7 Visual language has been analysed and woven throughout. ☐
8 Clear structure (weave) and precise language have been used. ☐
9 Analysis is objective (does not include your opinion). ☐
10 Analysis is proofread and edited. ☐

Practice activities

1 Devise your own *plan of attack* for the exam.

2 Practise your exam skills by completing both the 2012 and 2013 exams in Chapters 8 and 11, using your plan of attack timing and exam conditions.

3 There are also seven language analysis tasks at the end of Chapter 4.

Chapter 8

Suggested responses to VCAA exams 2008–2011

Suggested response to VCAA 2008 English exam

***A word from our coach …* [VCAA 2008 English exam]**
The issue of good sportsmanship allows a coach from a local sports club to address the larger issue of 'good' parent versus 'bad' parent and the effect on children and the club, in the new season's first newsletter, after poor sportsmanship in the previous seas has discouraged volunteers. Coach Sam contends in his column that 'the only goal that should matter in kids' sport is the promotion of good sportsmanship' and that parents have a responsibility to role model good behaviour 'before, during and after the game'. Coach Sam uses his experience and position together with a confident tone, informal style and accompanying cartoon to explain the importance of good sportsmanship to his target audience of parents.

Coach Sam opens his column with an anecdote in italics about eight-year-old 'distraught' Emily, whose 'dad yelled at her' for failing to 'save the game', undermining the credibility of 'aggressive' spectators and provoking readers to respond with protests against such treatment of a child. Cartoonist, Parker, mirrors this with the small, innocent girl in his cartoon bearing a flag; 'Team' is completely overshadowed by the aggressive donkey, reinforcing Coach Sam's idea that the merits of team spirit are being squashed by parents who are only focused on their child's role in winning the game.

Directly following the anecdote, Coach Sam uses strong language and divides parents into two categories: 'toxic parents' who suffer from 'sports rage' and 'are poisoning our club' versus the 'best' or 'good' parents who model and encourage good sportsmanship. In doing this he appeals to parents who wish to display good parenting skills as well as parental fears that the well-being of their sports club is threatened.

Using bold subheadings and rhetorical questions like 'What sort of parent are you?' throughout his column, Coach Sam makes his main points very clear to parents and challenges their thinking and actions. His constant use of 'we' and 'our' appeals to the parents' sense of community and pride in belonging to the club.

He first defines good sportsmanship using well-known examples like 'applauding good play', 'shaking hands' and recalling the 'Olympic runner who stopped to help his rival' to highlight to parents the role of 'both small gestures and heroic efforts'. Coach Sam acknowledges that 'displaying good sportsmanship isn't always easy' and likens the effort to a 'triumph of human spirit'.

He urges parents to 'be reasonable' and points out to the reader the repercussions or 'negative effect' of some parents' poor or 'loutish' behaviour in the previous season. Coach Sam states that 'hard-working volunteers [are] leaving the club disgusted' and 'coaches will hang up their whistles'. Following on from that argument he urges angry parents to 'have a go at me [Coach Sam]' implying that parents who 'take it out on the kids' are cowards. The cartoon highlights the dichotomy between 'good' parents and sports-aggressive 'bad' parents. The 'toxic parent' not 'accepting' a referee's call 'gracefully' is depicted by Parker as the spectators would see him: a large donkey prominently positioned and overshadowing the spectators, making them uncomfortable physically as well as emotionally. The donkey wears a T-shirt with the logo 'death is defeat', which emphasises to the reader the wrong importance placed on winning. The stunned and angry reactions from the other spectators, referee, scorers and two players to the abusive outburst are shown on their faces. Parker uses a speech bubble to voice a parent wishing that 'these sports-aggressive parents could see themselves as we do!', informing the reader that toxic parents lack insight into their own behaviour, are seen by other spectators as idiots, and spoil the game for everyone. Such a confronting image, like Coach Sam firmly states, shows that this parental behaviour is unacceptable and not in the spirit of the game. It is likely to provoke readers into taking steps to rectify the problem.

His last main point exhorts parents to 'be a good sport' and argues that they 'have a responsibility' to behave appropriately 'before, during and after the game'. He emphasises to parents that 'winning is just one of several goals' and the cartoon placed in this section of his column is a strong and confronting visual depiction of this point of view.

Coach Sam ends his column with deliberate use of the cliché, 'actions speak louder than words', reiterates the importance of 'your [parents'] behaviour during matches' and firmly places the responsibility of developing good sportsmanship in the hands of the parents.

Coach Sam's experience in the field, his clear argument, accessible examples and informal style together with Parker's in-your-face cartoon may succeed, where others have failed, in convincing parents to not tolerate unsportsmanlike behaviour and its negative effect on children and the club. Even if he does not succeed in converting 'toxic parents', his message is likely to appeal to all parents who take pride in the club as well as recognise the importance and value of good sportsmanship on and off the court.

Suggested response to VCAA 2009 English exam

Keyed In

In an opinion piece, *Keyed In*, for online journal *Ctrl Alt* and posted in response to debate about the impact of digital technology, Voxi contends that the impact of digital technology is a positive one and that it is 'an exciting tool of the modern world' that enables one to become 'faster', 'more efficient' and 'connected'. Voxi combines a conversational and confident tone with figurative and inclusive language, comparisons, popular examples and visuals to appeal to her audience of online readers who are 'digital savvy'.

Voxi begins by stating that there are two groups with polar views on the issue. She refers to one group as 'some people', then negatively describes them to her readers as 'suspicious', 'afraid', 'predictable' and 'safe', 'older people' and finally as 'losers'. In contrast, Voxi refers to the second group as 'other people' and positively describes them as 'excited' wanting to 'grab the future', 'adventurous', wanting to 'move forward', positioning the reader to identify with the 'other people' group throughout her opinion piece.

Voxi further describes digital technology users as 'gritty people' who 'produce pearls' and invent things, and includes references to historical figures such as 'Copernicus' and 'Galileo', which may flatter online readers by association. She also compares the advent of digital technology to other historical moments of discovery such as the discovery of the telescope and microscope, appealing to the online readers' sense of importance.

The selected sentences contained in the podcast extract discuss the 'so-called plasticity' of the brain and highlight to the reader the irrational fear of digital technology held by 'some people' who, Voxi claims, feel that it 'will reduce human intelligence … displace cognitive function with an artificial intelligence'.

Voxi refutes this school of thought by using it to expound her theory 'that by connecting digital technology and the human brain, human beings can become even more intelligent', prefacing her theory with the inclusive 'others can appreciate', confidently assuming that she is sharing her theory with like-minded readers.

The translucent digital image included in the piece is a visual representation of Voxi's 'homo supersapiens' and has a futuristic feel. It features computer chips glowing with binary codes exploding out of a human head and reinforces the claim that the human brain will become more powerful if connected to digital technology. This image is likely to appeal to users of digital technology because of its futuristic feel but may frighten 'some people' who are worried about people becoming less human because of digital technology, because they may feel that the image looks more robotic than human.

Voxi argues that digital technology is 'the exciting tool of the modern world' and links it to the common future dreams of mankind. Placing the rhetorical question, 'Why wouldn't you want it in your life?', after the 'dream' list of obvious positives, such as 'solve riddles of the universe, preserving the planet, ending war ... ', emphasises disbelief and makes it difficult for the reader to refute the potential digital technology offers for 'enhancing our lives'.

By listing current and popular examples of digital technology use such as 'global shopping', 'Google Maps' and 'Facebook', Voxi further polarises her readers and appeals to the younger generation who already access some digital technology and want to be thought of as modern, 'optimistic' and 'future thinking'. This may also serve to exclude readers who are 'older people who are less familiar with it' and may be 'even afraid'.

Voxi dismisses concerns about privacy issues related to digital technology, claiming that readers can 'protest about them anyway', 'get them removed or pixelated if [they] are really worried', implying that readers who do worry are concerned unnecessarily.

In conclusion, Voxi reiterates her point about digital technology users being 'excited' and positive about future discoveries at the same time as denigrating people who do not ascribe to her theory by likening them to cave people. Voxi generalises their view and claims that they consider 'new things are harmful or dangerous or unpredictable', implying that they impede humanity's progress.

Voxi's constant use of 'we' and 'our' together with a confident tone and positive spin on all aspects of digital technology are likely to appeal to her 'digital savvy' readers who are flattered to see themselves as 'heading for the 22nd century in a spirit of optimism'. Her piece, however, may alienate readers who are Luddites and readers who use some digital technology but do not agree that there are only two schools of thought on this issue.

Suggested response to VCAA 2009 EAL exam

Keyed In

Part 1

Issue: impact of digital technology
Auth: Voxi
Form: post – online journal *Ctrl Alt*
Aud: online readers/net users
Context: post about debate
Contention: impact of digital tech is +ve

**describes 2 types of people
1 'some people' = 'old', 'afraid', 'suspicious', 'loser', 'safe', 'predicable' against D tech
2 other people = 'adventurous', 'excited' for D tech

For (+ve)	Against (−ve)
D tech ➔ improved lives – 'microscope' 'telescope' (compare)	Challenges, opposes idea (incl podcast)
D tech rev way we comm	'Hot air balloon' (vis image) rebuts privacy issue
D tech + brains = smarter pers eg (vis lang) head + computer chip = bigger brain	'Buy a stack of stationery' = 'loser' (infers old fashioned, live in past)
advs = $, hols, maps, Facebook, peace etc (appeals to Net users)	
Tech is tool to solve probs and achieve future dreams, e.g. 'we can find cures faster', 'preserving planet', 'end war and violence' (list, incl lang)	
'why wouldn't you want that in your life?' (rhet Q)	
D tech means 'faster', 'efficient', 'more connected' = futuristic (appeals to mod thinkers)	

Part 2

In her online journal, *Keyed In*, Voxi believes that digital technology has a positive impact on the world and that there are two types of thinking about digital technology. Using a confident tone, she argues that digital technology is a 'tool to achieve future dreams' and includes examples of positive advantages of digital technology in an attempt to strengthen her point of view that digital technology should be embraced.

Voxi divides the world into two types of people: 'some people' and 'other people'. She describes 'some people' negatively as 'old', 'suspicious', 'afraid' of digital technology and, finally, as 'losers', who would rather 'buy a stack of stationery' than use a computer. Readers who are elderly or hesitant to embrace digital technology may feel hopeless or 'even afraid' after reading the loaded language. In contrast, Voxi describes the 'other people' as 'adventurous', 'excited' and who 'want to grab the future with both hands'. These words appeal to readers who wish to be considered as modern thinkers.

Voxi suggests that there may be benefits to digital technology. First, she claims that, 'by using digital technology and the human brain together, humans can become more intelligent'. The accompanying visual showing a futuristic digital image shows glowing computer chips with binary codes exploding out of a human head and reinforces this claim as the human brain looks powerful. This image is likely to delight users of technology but may frighten 'some people' who are worried about people becoming less human because of digital technology.

Finally, Voxi describes digital technology as 'the tool to achieve' modern world dreams of being able to 'find cures faster, find ways of preserving the planet, end war and violence' and states that 'we need dreams'. Readers are likely to be impressed by the potential of digital technology and excited about its future uses. In addition, Voxi emphasises that digital technology is about 'getting faster', 'being more efficient' and being 'connected'. She lists the positive advantages of 'global shopping', 'online banking', 'Google Maps' and 'Facebook', which appeals to readers who currently use this technology.

Suggested response to VCAA 2010 English exam

Biodiversity

The 2002 commitment to achieve a 'significant reduction in the rate of biodiversity loss' by 2010 has prompted a review of the progress achieved in order to 'take stock' and promote a sustainable future at the Nagoya Conference in Japan. Professor Chris Lee, in his keynote speech at the International Biodiversity Conference, contends in an increasingly concerned tone that 'our failure to conserve and use biological diversity in a sustainable manner is resulting in environmental degradation, new and more rampant illnesses, deepening poverty and a continuing pattern of inequitable and untenable growth on a global scale'. He attempts to convince his audience, international delegates, that immediate action is required by all.

Opening his keynote speech with a collegial and inclusive salutation, 'Ladies and gentlemen', Lee immediately asserts the formality of not only his presentation but the conference as a whole. The opening slide of Lee's presentation, 'Taking Stock', defines what is at stake if biodiversity is not protected and promotes its benefits in a calm and optimistic manner. The icon '2010' is created through blank silhouettes of fish, waves, birds, a tree, and a parent and child. The image subtly conveys the importance of harmonious interactions between the four different elements of life by including sea life, land life, plant life and human beings within the image. This reinforces for the delegates what is at risk if biodiversity is not protected and thus prepares them for Lee's didactic statement, 'This is a year of vital significance to our world'. Similarly, the italicised line 'Taking Stock' has strong connotations with consumerism and underlines Lee's condemnation of 'economic giants'.

Lee invites the audience's consternation and involvement in the issue by asking them to reflect on whether this has been achieved through the use of repetitious questions, 'has this', followed by the pertinent and revealing question, 'honestly, how well have we done?' The use of the word 'honestly' is preceded by the inclusive statement 'over the next two days we will be reviewing our progress', which serves to strengthen and unify the purpose of the conference and asserts the collective responsibility of the delegates present for the biodiversity problems which exist. This is reinforced by Lee's embedded clause 'indeed to strengthen' future goals, which highlights the collective goal of the delegates and the importance of immediate action. Lee challenges the collective responsibility he has established by acknowledging individual concern: 'one may justly ask'. The singular 'one' combines with the emotive 'justly' to compound the issue, implying one deeply concerned with humanity, and is reinforced by his acknowledgement of the 'idealistic' nature of the task he intends to do.

There is a tonal shift in the mid section of the speech – after Lee has established the purpose for the conference, Lee's tone shifts to being increasingly alarming. He introduces alarming statistics: 'we have lost 35% of mangroves, 40% of forests and 50% of wetlands', to mirror his tone selection. Delegates are given further cause for concern as authority figures, in this case 'IUCN', are utilised to add reliability and merit to Lee's statistics. The scientific nature of Lee's argument is countered by the short sentence 'It is too late for them', which is powerful and allows the delegates to see the loss not only from a numerical perspective but as the tragedy it is.

The 'truth' regarding the situation is magnified by references to 'the dinosaurs' disappear[ance]'. The argument culminates in not just lowered biodiversity but the terrifying prospect of 'extinction'. The use of the verb 'driven' places responsibility firmly on the collective 'we' that Lee is addressing. Furthermore, by tying his concern to 'human wellbeing' the delegates' fears are further heightened as the 'extinction' is now connected with humans also.

Lee continues by disallowing any excuses for the present state of lowered biodiversity. 'We know this', 'we are … the most educated generation' and 'we have no excuse' are exacerbated by the repetitious use of 'lack', and the telling concern regarding the 'lack of genuine commitment'. Lee apportions blame and invites the delegates to take responsibility for the current situation, which is described as 'grim'. The deliberate use of the word 'grim' has strong connotations with death as many delegates would immediately think of the grim reaper and in doing so Lee has reiterated the dire nature of the problem in the mind of the audience.

Lee deliberately makes delegates uncomfortable by describing their current approach as 'haphazard', which has strong associations with mistakes and poor planning. Lee increases the delegates' level of discomfort by juxtaposing 'real action' with 'wonderful words, glossy brochures, inspiring documentaries', which is designed to highlight the inaction of current approaches. Lee's tone emerges as attacking as he highlights the inadequacies of action designed from an 'air conditioned and sumptuously catered conference hall' as they inevitably become 'faint promises' and 'talk-fests'. This serves to ensure that delegates take responsibility and change their current strategies as they are embarrassed by their failed actions. This is insured through Lee's emphasised words 'WE', 'YOU' and 'YOUR country' which defines where blame lies.

Lee's argument shifts as he outlines the consequences of lowered biodiversity. His acknowledgement to prior knowledge 'There is no need to remind you' and 'As we all know' appeals to the delegates' intellect. This is furthered through specific vocabulary choices 'inequitable', 'untenable' and 'rampant illnesses', which promote concern and highlight the unequal impact of lowered biodiversity on a 'global scale'. As responsibility is fostered for collective action globally for those who 'are not in a position to do anything about it', Lee places a 'face' on the victims: 'poor rural communities'. By generating human concern for a scientific problem, Lee has increased the audience's concern. Continuing by highlighting those at risk as 'vulnerable' Lee connects biodiversity with economics. The critical and informal term 'affluenza' counters the scientific and financial jargon in order to highlight how the problem may be solved if personal interests are ignored by 'the interests of us, the powerful economic giants'. By including himself in the statement, Lee alleviates the offence some may feel in being labelled as responsible due to their wealth. By linking our modern 'affluent' behaviour with our primal and instinctive behaviours as 'hunters and gatherers', Lee is able to further alleviate individual guilt because the cause of the problem has been instinctive behaviour; this then allows for listeners to see the urgency of immediate collective action and the importance of changing current behaviours before it is 'too late!'.

In concluding with a reassertion of Lee's faith in the delegates' intellect – 'Is any of this new information? ... Of course not!' – and reminding them of their role as 'leaders', Lee makes one final appeal to them for 'serious action'. By targeting those in control – 'politicians ... corporate leaders' – the 'everyday householder' has been given the correct mechanisms for doing so. Lee ensures that the delegates are left with the task of promoting 'serious action'. His keynote address is closed with the words of ecologist Thomas Eisner, which reasserts his contention, 'Biodiversity is the greatest treasure we have ... Its diminishment is to be prevented at all costs' and reaffirms Lee's stance on the issue through the use of expert opinion. The quote appears on the closing slide of Lee's presentation, which is reinforced through the image of a female holding the world. The female hands suggest 'mother nature', promote a sense of care for the Earth and promote its fragility, through the gentle hold the hands have on the world. The globe presented is positioned so that Africa is centred for the audience, reminding delegates one final time what is at risk, 'poor rural communities', and really illustrates the world as the 'treasure' Eisner asserts it is.

The closing words 'thank you' ensure delegates feel their time and their efforts have been appreciated and ensures that the delegates are more likely to take the 'serious action' Lee requires of them so that they are not responsible for further extinctions.

Suggested response to VCAA 2010 EAL exam

Biodiversity

Part 1

Biodiversity 2002–2010

[living things and places and relationship bw them]

reduction in biodiversity reduces poverty +ve benefit for Earth

Damage = we've done b/c rich lifestyle	**Need to do = action**
1 Enviro, e.g. • mangrove < 35% • forests < 40% • wetlands < 50% 2 Disease – fast spreading 3 Animals become extinct, e.g. 100 × natural rate 4 Inequality global wealth ↓ poverty = 1.1 billion	• Our responsibility ↓ world in our hands [closing slide] • change rich lifestyles • reverse -ve trend • set goals • must act ≠ not talk ↓ send messages to pollies, biz leaders, householders

Part 2

In his speech at the Nagoya conference, Professor Chris Lee contends that we have 'failed in our commitment to achieve significant reduction in the rate of biodiversity loss'. He uses inclusive language and repeated rhetorical questions throughout the speech, 'Honestly, how well have we done?', 'How much have we really done?' and 'What have WE – what have YOU and YOUR country – actually done since 2002 to help achieve our goals?' The combination of inclusive language and rhetorical questions may prompt the audience to consider their own role in 'environmental damage', 'fast-spreading illnesses' and 'increasing poverty'. Here, Lee appeals to the audience's sense of responsibility and humanity, hoping they will change their current approach.

The opening slide in Lee's presentation is a visual representation of the biodiversity definition and demonstrates the positive interaction between man, animals and natural habitat. From the outset, Lee establishes an optimistic tone and urges the audience to celebrate 'biodiversity in our lives'. However, Lee's tone changes to a fearful one when he lists the 'failures to conserve' and 'preserve biodiversity'. He outlines 'environmental damage', 'fast-spreading illnesses' and 'increasing poverty' as potential dangers to civilisation and supports them with damning statistics: 'lost 35% of mangroves, 40% of forests and 50% of wetlands' and 'plants and animals becoming extinct' 'up to 100 times the rate of natural extinction'. Both the ominous tone and disturbing statistics are designed to unsettle the audience, who will immediately worry about the potential threats to their well-being.

Lee concludes his presentation with ecologist Thomas Eisner's message, 'Biodiversity is the greatest treasure we have ... Its diminishment is to be prevented at all costs'. This idea is further strengthened by Lee's closing slide depicting a world in female hands. Not only do these sentiments tie into the concluding line of Lee's speech, but they also act as a call to action for the audience of delegates, showing them that they have the power to change the situation. Once again, Lee appeals to the audience's sense of duty and tells them 'now, truly, is the time for serious action', and 'We must reinforce this message to those in power'. His final 'Thank you' is in response to his audience's concern and likely to encourage the audience to feel compelled to take 'serious action'.

Suggested responses to the VCAA 2011 English exams

Section C – Analysis of language use

Mainstream response

Helen Day's popular blog, *Street Beat*, has used social media to discuss the changing attitudes towards tattoos. In her post, 'The Power of Ink', Day contends in an authoritative and confident tone that the tattoo has lost its connotations of 'deviance' and 'criminality' as they have become 'a fashion statement'. Day appeals to her 12 615 strong readership and targets younger readers in particular through her language choices and accompanying visuals aimed at causing her blog followers to think before getting tattoos for trivial reasons. The four comments in response to Day's post use a range of tones from upbeat to hurtful as they variously claim that tattoos are 'unique', not 'individual', culturally significant and have associated medical risks. Three of the comments clearly support Day's point of view as an older person while Tash's comment exemplifies Day's earlier thinking about tattoos.

The title of the blog entry, 'The Power of Ink', is ironic as Day argues that the tattoo has lost its 'power' to commonality. The bold sentence at the start of her piece outlines her contention and allows her to foreshadow the historical context of her argument from 'once a sign' to 'now'. Immediately appealing to her youthful followers, Day begins with an inclusive statement – 'Everyone has a tattoo these days' – which is compounded by her own authority, 'even me', which establishes not only her experience regarding tattoos but also her own familiarity with her audience. This ties in with the hyperlink the 'ABOUT ME' section of her blog, which furthers her audience's ability to identify with her. The appeal to youth is continued through the reference to a 'mega shopping centre', later 'try hard', and the unattractive image of 'suburban housewives' who are likened to 'prison[ers]'. The increasingly unattractive image of people with ill-planned tattoos is magnified as Day contrasts her audience with 'newsreaders, sitcom stars and upmarket shoppers' who she identifies as having 'diminished' the power of the tattoo. This serves to not alienate her audience as their desire for a tattoo has been compromised by others, not themselves. Her inclusion of the book cover, *No tattoos before you're thirty. What I'll tell my children,* highlights the trivial, meaningless tattoos which are symbolic of youthful carelessness and have not been thought through properly. The isolated shoulder featured renders the tattoo as aggressive; furthermore, the title of the book creates a dichotomy between youthful stupidity and the wisdom generated from experience.

There is a tonal shift as Day generates a historical context for her contemporary audience. The short, sharp sentence 'It was not always so' is isolated to signpost the reflective and, in places, condemning nature of Day's argument regarding 'earliest times' and tattoos' symbolic meaning. Day employs a photograph to highlight the duality associated with tattoos' meaning. The image of the Ta Moko tattoo from the three different angles is a proud symbol of masculine identity which clearly has strong connotations with culture and is an expression of belonging. This image strengthens the rationality of Day's argument.

The use of politically unattractive terms such as 'slaves' appeals to Day's readership's conscience as her references to the 'unconsenting' prisoners who were 'incarcerated' or 'deviant' undermines the 'fashion[able]' nature of tattoos, causing Day's audience to reconsider their own desire to get a tattoo. This is compounded by the reference to 20th century history and the 'genocide' of the Holocaust, as the 'horror' of this part of our recent history is designed to modify Day's argument and prove its validity across many centuries.

Day's argument becomes increasingly academic as she again employs history to look at the changing attitudes towards tattoos. However, she presents the timeline of ownership through to acceptance, in order to reiterate that the experiences of the past indicate that tattoos have tragically lost their meaning. The argument relating to the 'crown' contrasts the 'King' with the aggressive verb 'flogged' in order to show defiance as an important part of Australian history and, indeed, identity. Day's argument shifts as she relies primarily on her own experience as both an 'angry young thing' and a woman. By employing the language that adults often do to belittle teenagers and young adults, Day immediately shows her understanding of the complexity of the issue and the reasons why people feel that they should get tattoos. This is counteracted by the anger she feels about the 'sexy' nature of the modern tattoo and their commonness, 'even adorn', which lead her to feel profoundly annoyed by her own tattoo, which she feels 'stuck ... with' rather than seeing it as a symbol of her youthful liberation.

Day concludes with her contention, 'The tattoo has become commodified ... it is fashion's proprietary mark'. She carefully ties this bleak interpretation to her own decisions and carefully ensures that she doesn't offend her audience, who may have tattoos, by acknowledging the cultural abandon she once felt 'unfolding on [her] skin'; however, ultimately it has been reduced to 'any other cosmetic quirk'. The final sentence combines the assonance of 'ornament', 'ordinary' and 'other', and contrasts it with the alliterative 'cosmetic quirk' to allow readers to comprehend the sharp change in the tattoo's status in modern history.

Day's blog invites commentary from her audience to increase engagement and debate within her social media. The language of her audience varies strongly as each member passionately contends their point of view on the issue. Tash argues strongly that her tattoo makes her 'unique'. Employing colloquial language, 'No way!', 'and yeah' and 'my mum was rapt', Tash allows for a wide support base for her argument and presents a youthful image generating understanding for her argument. This contrasts strongly with Dr AB, whose clinical and authoritative argument regarding the medical risks associated with tattoos employs medical and practical language 'permanent' and 'pigment' to increase the validity of his argument. The health scares listed – 'bleeding, hepatitis B, hepatitis C, tetanus, potentially significant pain, and a pus-like drainage' – may generate fear within readers and cause concern for personal safety. This is designed to counteract any hedonistic arguments generated in support of tattoos. The irony and humour utilised by Cleanskin – 'so many dolphins have faded and stretched into whales' – uses unattractive imagery to counter aesthetic desires for tattoos. This furthered by Cleanskin's use of the word 'rebel', which he associates with being individual enough not to have a tattoo. His use of the derogatory term 'hack' reinforces Dr AB's point about associated medical risks.

In the closing post, Kiwi highlights the cultural significance of the tattoo for his family and heritage. The hurtful tone of his argument that imitation of cultural tattoos is akin to 'identity theft' ties to Day's photograph and caption of Ta Moko and strengthens the concerns Day has highlighted in her blog. The closing question, 'How would you feel if someone stole those from you?' addresses the readers directly and forces them to question the 'morality' of future tattoos, and invites them to consider avoiding the temptation to get one for fashionable reasons, as tattoos should be an item of significance for all who have one.

Day's blog post and readers' comments discuss the issue of the significance and power of tattoos. Day concludes her argument with the realisation that while tattoos are now commonplace, some tattoos are special and have 'cultural significance'. The responses reinforce aspects of her argument and are likely to encourage her followers to think twice about getting a tattoo.

EAL Section C – Analysis of language use

Part 1 response

Topic: Tattoos: Power of Ink

Audience: *Street Beat* blog followers = late teens and early 20s. 12 615 (large number), 'us', 'we' 'our'
Form: blog = personal, her feelings. her story, e.g. 'I', 'personally', 'about me'
Author: Helen Day, p/time journo and blogger, 'young woman' when got tatt (rebel 'activist youth')
Tone: confident

Tattoos
BEFORE -ve ➔sign of control (Greeks, Romans, Conc. Camps) ➔ rebellion/defiance 18C-UK, 20C
➔NOW +ve common, 'ordinary'
HOWEVER still special 'mark of belonging' = cultural ID

— criminals, ownership and med facts	+ve sign = diff and rebellion	Now = common and +ve cultural ID
1 sign of ownership 2 crims -ve mark of belonging e.g. Hist facts • Greek and Roman slaves, prisoners • Europe mid ages = prisoners, deviant • WWII conc. camps • Shock reaction 3 *Dr AB – tattoo med dangers = skin infects, hep B, C, tet and pain	1 sign of diff symbol of rebellion • 18C convicts 'Property of Eng' (fact) • 'no tattoos before you're 30'= parents say • HD e.g. 20C – 1990s 'tatt shops' = 'fast food outlets' • 'Angry young women' had gender tats (fem symbols)	1 fashion statement, 'ordinary' 'cosmetic peculiarity' 2 +ve 'mark of belonging' e.g. tatt symbols ➔Ta Moko (Maori cult) Vis 1 ➔ 'signature' no shock reaction
100% 🡐 POWER OF TATTS SHOCK VALUE 0% ➔ 0%		

Part 2 response

In her *Street Beat* blog about the social issue of the power of tattoos, part-time journalist Helen Day, contends that the power of tattoos has decreased in 'shock value' from being a negative 'sign of ownership, brutality and trouble' through to an act of defiance through to a positive 'mark of belonging' of cultural identity and 'ordinary' cosmetic peculiarity that is commonplace. She employs a variety of historical, cultural and medical facts, visual images and personal knowledge to convince her audience of followers that 'everyone has tattoos these days'. Day appeals to her large following of 12 615 people using a confident tone, inclusive language and personal writing style.

Day opens her entry with a personal example and discusses her own tattoo as an act of 'defiance' gotten as a 'symbol of my rebellion' by a young woman. She uses inclusive language such as 'we', 'our' and 'us' to connect to her readers. Day argues that because tattoos are so commonplace now the 'symbol of my rebellion' is now 'as ordinary as any other cosmetic peculiarity'. This argument is reinforced by the photograph of a tattooed arm with the body text, 'No tattoos before you're thirty' and smaller font 'What I'll tell my children …'. It says to the reader that, years later, because the power of the tattoo has decreased, what was once an act of defiance is now seen differently. Her claim that it is now seen as 'ordinary' is both a personal and powerful example of how the power of ink has 'faded'. Consequently, the readers who are drawn to tattoos for their shock value may feel disappointed knowing that they are no longer a sign of rebellion.

Day includes researched historical facts to establish the once negative association of criminals and ownership with tattoos with Greeks and Romans who 'inked the backs of unconsenting prisoners and slaves' and the powerful image of 'identification numbers' tattooed on the arms of World War II concentration camp survivors. She also highlights medical problems, including Dr AB's warning that tattoos 'can cause bleeding, hepatitis B, hepatitis C, tetanus, significant pain and infection'. The reader is likely to feel fearful of the problems associated with tattoos, which they may have been unaware of.

Day concludes her argument with her realisation that while tattoos are now commonplace, some tattoos are special and have 'cultural significance'. Her photograph of Ta Moko used in Maori culture provides visual evidence of this fact. The caption refers to the practice as 'body art' which shows that the wearer's 'status' and 'family heritage' are a 'sacred form of family and personal identification'. Three different arms with the same tattoos reinforces the strong image of positive cultural identify or 'mark of belonging' to the reader.

Chapter 9

VCAA 2012 English exams

Section C – Analysis of language use

Instructions for Section C

Section C requires students to analyse the ways in which language and visual features are used to present a point of view.

Section C is worth one-third of the total assessment for the examination.

Read the following material and then complete the task below.

Write your analysis as a coherently structured piece of prose.

Your response will be assessed according to the criteria set out in this book.

TASK

How is written and visual language used to attempt to persuade the audience to share the point of view of the speaker?

Background information

- The following pages contain the transcript of a speech by Mrs Elliot, a retired teacher--librarian, at the opening of 'Reading: the Future', a forum on reading and literacy-related activities.
- Two slides used by the speaker during her presentation are also shown.
- The audience included teachers, librarians and senior school students from local schools.

Good morning fellow book-lovers.

I have always been what's known as an 'early adopter', someone who is enthusiastic about new technology.

As a teenager I was excited to learn about the massive change that hit the world when Gutenberg invented the first printing press in the 15th century. Until then, books were extremely precious and rare objects made by hand and owned only by the rich, but with this new machine they could be produced again and again. The number of books in the world exploded.

I like change. So when electronic books arrived, I rushed out to buy an e-reading device. I thought making books easier to get, cheaper to own and more convenient to carry had to be a good thing. I wanted to be free of the expense that goes with a lifetime of book-buying, and I wanted effortless library borrowing and effortless return of books. I imagined children setting off to school without the terrible burden of their great big textbooks.

Like many of you I'm an enthusiastic reader and I see books as a doorway to other worlds – worlds that we actively create in our imaginations, using someone else's words.

My enthusiasm extends to e-books. Some things about them are great. I love being able to change the brightness settings and the font size; it's fun to look up a dictionary or Wikipedia just by selecting a word. And it's exciting to know that e-books can break through the limitations of the printing press.

So what's to worry about?

Well, I do wonder about the video and animated images that some e-books will contain. They might become a kind of substitute for genuine reading. Recently I saw a TV ad showing a child, all alone, looking at a tablet device. At first I thought he was reading, but he wasn't. He was viewing – some might say 'experiencing' – computer-generated images of dinosaurs. I don't find this exciting. To me it's disturbing, the idea of a child passively consuming something already imagined and packaged up in a conveniently portable form, as empty and unwholesome as a packet of potato chips. Those dinosaurs didn't spring to life in his imagination. They existed only in a high-speed wireless connection, without which they would be as dead as … well, dinosaurs.

A slide from the presentation

Source: photo.ua/shutterstock.com

And I wonder about endless exposure to screens. Do we really think it will be healthy for our kids to spend hours and hours using e-books at school, on top of the time they already spend watching TV or playing electronic games? And will we then think it's okay for them to take an e-book to bed? My generation used to laugh at our parents for trying to limit the hours we spent watching TV. That doesn't seem so silly now.

One of the things I love most about reading is the magical way it allows us to see impossible or unreal things in our imaginations, making the boring everyday world disappear completely for a while. But I was shocked to discover that some e-books might disappear in a puff of smoke themselves. Publishers have in mind to update textbooks every year as knowledge changes. That sounds exciting, but it means you mightn't get to keep your textbooks permanently. Unless you paid every year, they'd vanish, recalled by the publisher and software owner. You couldn't sell them at the community second-hand bookstore. And when something went out of e-print, how would you ever find it again?

No wonder there's a move by concerned book-lovers to build huge warehouses to preserve bound books. They fear the loss of knowledge, history, even culture itself, as the world is flooded with e-books that are accessible only through special software and that depend on the computer servers of the World Wide Web. If global cyber disaster struck, the loss would be unthinkable.

A slide from the presentation

Source: J Wheeler

I have a fear, too, that e-books might increase the gap between rich and poor. Knowledge and education are a form of wealth. I hope expensive, energy-hungry e-reading devices don't become a new way of keeping some people ignorant, as in the bad old days before mass print technology made books cheaper.

Recently I took the final Harry Potter story on a long and unpleasant flight to London, hoping it would shorten the trip. I opened the book and it worked! The plane, my fellow passengers, Earth below, instantly ceased to exist. Time itself began to fly.

In London I left the book in a red telephone box for anyone passing by who happened to want to read it. I felt a bit like a Harry Potter character myself, being able to make a free book appear from nowhere. By contrast, my e-books, which arrive by the modern wizardry of the internet, just sit silently on their virtual shelf when they're finished, instead of being part of the lending and sharing that traditionally goes on between people who love books.

Now I'm starting to sound a bit like a dinosaur myself, aren't I?

Nothing can stop the coming of e-books and I wouldn't want to stop it. I'll go on being an early adopter of new technology and new ways. But all of us who care about reading, and you young people as future leaders, we must all do what we can, as this revolution rolls over us, to make sure that important things are not entirely swept away.

Examination assessment criteria

The examination will address all the criteria. Student responses will be assessed against the following criteria.

Section C – Analysis of language use

- understanding of the ideas and points of view presented
- analysis of ways in which language and visual features are used to present a point of view and to persuade readers
- controlled and effective use of language appropriate to the task

EAL Section C – Analysis of language use

Instructions for Section C

Section C consists of **two** parts.

Part 1 and 2 are equally weighted.

Section C is worth 30 marks.

Carefully read the material below and then complete **both** parts 1 and 2.

Your response will be assessed according to the criteria set out in this book.

TASK

Part 1
Write a note-form summary of the speech by Mrs Elliot. Your response must be in **note form**. Do not use complete sentences.

Part 2
Write a piece of prose that explains how language and visual features have been used in the speech by Mrs Elliot to attempt to persuade the audience about **three** of the main points in the speech.

Background information

- The following pages contain the transcript of a speech by Mrs Elliot. Mrs Elliot was speaking at the opening of 'Reading: The Future', a forum on reading and literacy-related activities. She is a retired teacher-librarian.
- Two slides used by the speaker during her presentation are also shown.
- The audience included teachers, librarians and senior school students from local schools.

Good morning fellow book-lovers.

I have always been enthusiastic about new technology.

As a teenager I was excited to learn about the massive change that hit the world when Gutenberg invented the first printing press in the 15th century. Until then, books were precious and rare objects, made by hand and owned only by the rich. With Gutenberg's new printing press multiple copies of books could be produced. The number of books in the world exploded.

I like change. So when electronic books arrived, I rushed out to buy an e-reading device. I thought making books easier to get, cheaper to own and more convenient to carry would be a good thing. I wanted to be free of the expense that goes with a lifetime of book-buying. I wanted instant borrowing instead of visiting the library to pick up books. I even imagined children setting off to school without the terrible burden of their great big textbooks.

Like many of you, I'm an enthusiastic reader. I see books as a key to other worlds – worlds that we actively create in our imaginations, using someone else's words.

My enthusiasm extends to e-books. Some things about them are great. I love being able to change the brightness settings and the font size. It's fun to look up an e-dictionary or Wikipedia just by selecting a word. And it's exciting to know that e-books can contain more than printed books. They aren't just an electronic copy of the printed page – they can contain video and animated images.

So is there anything to worry about?

Well, I wonder whether the video and animated images of e-books will become a substitute for genuine reading. Recently I saw a TV advertisement showing a child, all alone, looking at a tablet device. At first I thought that he was reading, but he wasn't. He was viewing – some might say 'experiencing' – computer-generated dinosaurs. I don't find this exciting. To me it's just disturbing. He was passively consuming something imagined by someone else and packaged up like a takeaway meal. Those dinosaurs didn't come to life in his imagination. They existed only in a high-speed wireless connection, without which they would be as dead as … well, dinosaurs.

A slide from the presentation

[Source: photo.ua/shutterstock.com]

And I wonder about endless hours of exposure to screens. Do we really think it will be healthy for kids to spend hours and hours using e-books at school, in addition to the time they already spend watching TV or playing electronic games? My generation used to laugh at our parents for trying to limit the hours we spent watching TV. It doesn't seem so silly now.

What's more, I was shocked to discover that some e-books are not as permanent as printed books. Textbooks might be updated every year as knowledge changes. That sounds exciting, but it means you wouldn't own your textbooks anymore. If you wanted to keep them you would have to pay each year. Otherwise they would vanish, recalled by the publisher and software owner. You wouldn't be able to sell them at the community second-hand bookstore. And when something went out of e-print, how would you ever find it again?

It is not surprising that concerned book-lovers want to build huge warehouses to preserve printed books. They fear that knowledge, history, even culture itself, will be lost as the world is flooded with e-books that are accessible only through special software and the World Wide Web. If global cyber disaster struck, the loss of knowledge would be too terrible to think about.

A slide from the presentation

Source: J Wheeler

I have a fear, too, that e-books might increase the gap between rich and poor. Knowledge and education are a form of wealth. I hope expensive e-reading devices don't become a new way of keeping some people ignorant, as happened in the time before the printing press made books cheaper.

Recently, as I was walking in a park, I noticed a book that had been left on a seat. On the cover there was a sticker saying that the book had been left there deliberately. It was free for anyone to read and leave in another public place for another fellow reader. What a happy thought. A free book appearing from nowhere! By contrast, instead of being part of lending and sharing, e-books just sit on their virtual shelf when they are finished.

Now I'm starting to sound a bit like a dinosaur myself, aren't I?

Nothing can stop the coming of e-books and I wouldn't want to stop it. I will continue to be enthusiastic about new technology. But all of us who care about reading, and you young people as future leaders, we must all do what we can to make sure that important things are not entirely lost.

Examination assessment criteria

The examination will address all the criteria. Student responses will be assessed against the following criteria.

Section C – Analysis of language use

- understanding of the ideas and points of view in the material presented
- analysis of ways in which language and visual features are used to present a point of view and to persuade readers
- control of the mechanics of the English language to support meaning

Chapter 10

Suggested responses to the VCAA 2012 English exams

Section C – Analysis of language use

Mainstream response

As technology continues to develop and begins to encompass all aspects of life there is growing concern amongst some parts of the educational community regarding the sacrifices we may be inadvertently making. Mrs Elliot, a retired teacher–librarian, addresses this concern in her speech, which opened the 'Reading: The Future' forum. Her speech employs a rational yet in places fearful tone to convey to her audience (teachers, librarians and senior school students) that while 'nothing can stop the coming of e-books ... we must all do what we can ... to make sure that important things are not entirely swept away'.

Opening with a collegial and warm salutation, 'Good morning fellow book-lovers', Mrs Elliot quickly imbues her target audience with a sense of community, and as such they are invited to share her concern. This is compounded by the immediate use of the first person 'I' as Mrs Elliot references her personal reputation as an 'early adopter'. Her enthusiasm counters any reservations her audience may have about her stance due to her previous experience as a teacher–librarian and absolves her of any bias regarding her concern over the e-book 'revolution'. This is furthered by her personal reflections, 'As a teenager', which targets the student body in her audience and allows her to relate to them. Mrs Elliot appeals to the audience's nostalgia through her carefully placed adjectives 'precious' and 'rare', which highlights the craftsmanship associated with the creation of books. This nostalgia is contrasted with Mrs Elliot's confession 'I like change'. This is followed by three superlatives 'easier ... cheaper ... more', which are designed to convey not only Mrs Elliot's excitement but to reiterate her rational stance as she 'wanted effortless library borrowing and effortless return of books'.

Mrs Elliot mirrors her imagery of children going to school 'without the terrible burden of their great big textbooks' with a photograph of a school-aged child connected to an e-book leaning against a stack of thick books. This image presents Mrs Elliot's utopian desire for a world where the use of e-books complements daily life. The student is relaxed and facing the camera, and he is engaged in his reading; however, he is supported by the column of books. It is this combination that is appealing to Mrs Elliot's audience, fellow reading enthusiasts. She further heightens the impact of this image with the statement 'Like many of you', which involves them in both her enthusiasm and concern as this 'enthusiasm extends to e-books' allows her to recognise, by listing, the virtues of e-books. 'I love', 'It's fun' and 'it's exciting' are examples of hyperbole that develop her stance as an understanding and educated speaker in the eyes of the audience. This deepens the impact of the strong tonal shift brought about by the question, 'So what's to worry about?'

As her speech becomes increasingly fearful, Mrs Elliot employs a concerned tone conveyed by 'all alone', which contrasts with the 'precious' image of reading previously created. The previous 'excitement' is challenged by the didactic statement 'to me it's disturbing', which is cemented by the repeated references to 'dinosaurs', the most infamous case of extinction. By playing on this common knowledge and tying it to her audience's fear, 'they would be as dead as ... well, dinosaurs' Mrs Elliot highlights the subtle connection between mismanaged excitement and inadvertent sacrifices, and is likely to instil anxiety in her audience about potential losses. The simile 'as empty and unwholesome as a packet of potato chips' connects Mrs Elliot's concern for students and 'kids' with the other high-profile concern for Australia's youth: obesity. This sense of loss is exacerbated by the imagery provided in the repeated use of rhetorical questions of students 'spend[ing] hours and hours ... playing electronic games' and 'think[ing] it's okay for them to take an e-book to bed'. By tying these future fears with 'My generation' and the fears of previous ones, Mrs Elliot demonstrates the timelessness of concern and, thus, increases the validity of her argument as she recognises its cycle.

Mrs Elliot continues by presenting a positive reflection on the things she 'loves most about reading'. This is generated through the 'magical' power of escapism as she presents the 'impossible or unreal' feats reading lets readers accomplish. Mrs Elliot turns this magic around as she utilises magical terminology to illustrate the limitations of e-books, as they 'might disappear in a puff of smoke themselves' and she plays on the devastation that would be felt as the e-books 'vanished'. This dystopia is reinforced through the cartoon presented of a world that accepts 'vanish[ing]' possessions. The sacrifices embedded in the image, like gift wrapping and browsing, present the audience with a diminished consumer experience as people of all ages, as indicated by the cartoon, will lose if e-books take over books. This is linked to Mrs Elliot's 'fear' for the 'loss of knowledge, history, even culture itself', which, when combined with dangerous words 'flooded' and 'global cyber disaster', would very likely alarm her audience, causing them to think more carefully about what might be lost. This alarm is supported by a genuine concern for society as 'e-books might increase the gap between rich and poor'. Mrs Elliot invites her audience to connect this concern with an environmental one as 'energy-hungry' becomes associated with the rich and a form of discrimination.

Mrs Elliot closes her speech with an extended personal anecdote of her experience of reading Harry Potter on a long haul flight to London. The deliberate use of the literary world's most famous wizard allows Mrs Elliot to further her description of reading possessing magical properties as 'time itself began to fly'. Her magnanimous gesture of leaving the book in a telephone box is presented as an expression of her affection for the protagonist and desire to emulate him – 'I felt a bit like Harry Potter' – and presents her audience with another testament to the power of books. This generosity is presented as being at risk as e-books are presented as selfishly 'sit[ting] on their virtual shelf', which starkly contrasts with the 'lending and sharing that traditionally goes on between people who love books' and makes e-books seem even less appealing to her like-minded audience. Mrs Elliot increases her authenticity in the eyes of her audience as she admits to 'sound[ing] a bit like a dinosaur'. By returning to her previously established metaphor, Mrs Elliot gently reminds her audience of the dire consequences of change without caution: extinction.

Her final statement is both inclusive and balanced – 'I wouldn't want to stop it ... but all of us who care about reading' – and invites action from her audience. She targets the students in her audience – 'you young people as future leaders' – and combines their 'futures' with their need to act as a community in a logical appeal that 'we must all do what we can' in order to ensure that the positives of reading are 'not entirely swept away'. Ultimately her audience will be left with mixed feelings as those who were very optimistic about the potential of e-books to enhance reading might now be concerned at the possible associated losses with the new technology.

EAL Section C – Analysis of language use

Part 1 response

Reading: The Future
Mrs E (ret teach + lib)
F = speech. A = teach lib students
↓
ebooks (tech)
good + bad (probs)

+ve ←

- < $
- instant borrow
- < wght to carry (vis)
- Δ brightness + font size
- vid + animation
- edicty

→ **-ve**

- view ~~read~~
- no imagine
- > screen hrs = unhealthy
- no 2nd hand stores
- ~~permanent~~ (vis)

'lost' things
↓
cyber disaster → no ebooks
share + lend
↑gap b/w rich & poor
imagination??
↓
WARNING
ebooks = good
BUT
don't forget

Part 2 response

This transcript is of a speech on 'Reading: The Future' given by Mrs Elliot, a retired teacher–librarian, to teachers, librarians and senior school students.

In her speech Mrs Elliot contends that e-books are beneficial but that 'we must all do what we can to make sure that important things are not entirely lost'. She uses inclusive language, 'fellow book-lovers', to connect with her target audience. Mrs Elliot first outlines the positive aspects of e-books and new technology using a positive tone and photograph, and then introduces the negative aspects, changing her tone to concern as she reveals facts and a supporting cartoon. Finally, Mrs Elliot points out the 'fears' and warns her audience about the future.

Mrs Elliot opens her speech positively by describing herself as 'enthusiastic about technology' and saying that she 'rushed out to buy an e-reading device'. She refers to her excitement at the historical fact of Gutenberg's printing press.

She lists the advantages of e-books as ‘making books easier to get’, ‘cheaper’, ‘instant borrowing’, able to ‘change the brightness settings and font size’ and the video and animation making them ‘fun’. Her point about them being ‘more convenient to carry’ is supported by her first slide, a photograph of a happy, relaxed student using an e-reader with audio sitting against a stack of heavy textbooks, which shows that students no longer have the ‘terrible burden of their great big textbooks’. After hearing the benefits of the e-book, the audience is likely to feel excited about the advantages associated with the device.

Mrs Elliot introduces the negative aspects of e-books with a rhetorical question, ‘So is there anything to worry about?’ Using a concerned tone and language like ‘disturbing’, she questions whether ‘viewing’ will become a ‘substitute’ for reading. Here, the use of emotive language may arouse fear within the audience. In addition, Mrs Elliot likens the viewing experience to a ‘takeaway meal’, saying that the reader doesn’t actually read, and she also questions whether it is ‘healthy’ for students to spend ‘hours and hours using e-books at school’. Mrs Elliot is ‘shocked’ to find out that some e-books are not permanent like printed books and supports this point with a cartoon of a teenager buying a printed book and a caption emphasising how printed books remain in print longer than e-books.

Mrs Elliot concludes her speech by pointing out the possible important things that may be ‘lost’ due to e-books. ‘Concerned book-lovers’ fears that ‘knowledge, history and even culture’ will be lost and her ‘fear’ that e-books might ‘increase the gap between rich and poor’ just like in ‘the 15th century’. She also includes a ‘happy’ personal anecdote about a ‘free book’ being shared and contrasts it with e-books just sitting on ‘their virtual shelf’. Her last point is a warning to the ‘young people as future leaders’ in her audience saying that, ‘we must all do what we can to make sure that important things are not entirely lost’. Ultimately the audience will be left with mixed feelings. In this respect, some audience members may be optimistic regarding the e-book’s potential to enhance the reading process. Others may view the e-book with a degree of suspicion and be apprehensive about its introduction.

Chapter 11

VCAA 2013 English exams

Section C – Analysis of language use

Instructions for Section C

Section C requires students to analyse the ways in which language and visual features are used to present a point of view.

Read the following material and then complete the task below.

Write your analysis as a coherently structured piece of prose.

Your response will be assessed according to the criteria set out on in this book.

Section C is worth one-third of the total assessment for the examination.

TASK

How does the writer use written and visual language to attempt to persuade readers to share his point of view?

Background information

A community has been discussing possible future uses for an area of land that has not been used since the closure of a railway line. The local city council owns the land and is considering proposals for its use. The Grow Slow Garden Group has proposed that the land be used for the establishment of a community garden.

The leader of the Grow Slow Garden Group has produced a newsletter, as shown below. Before the council's decision is made, this newsletter will be distributed to every household in the local area.

Getting our future back on the rails – slowly

As just about everyone knows, the Council is about to decide what to do with the abandoned railway yards to the east of our central business area, land that is currently good only for rats, snakes and those few antisocial citizens who think it's acceptable to dump rubbish illegally. Soon, the shouting will be over. We hope the Council will decide in favour of a community garden, and we'll all be able to get behind the project and get it moving.

Everyone has had the chance to put forward ideas, including those who wanted the land fenced and concreted over and used for skateboarding or for yet another car park. But there has been a lot of misinformation and misguided comment, so this newsletter is to clear the air and set the record straight.

Some people who objected to the proposed garden seem to think the idea comes from a radical group of environmentalists. Grow Slow are proud to be contributing to a greener Australia, but there's nothing extreme about us. In fact it's high time the Council took notice of international trends and gave the community the go-ahead to transform this shockingly neglected wasteland into fresh, natural land.

This is a forward-thinking Council and it has the chance to bring us up to date with the rest of the world. City farms and cooperative, shared garden allotments are common in other countries. And they can be surprisingly productive. It might sound like a hobby but these small gardens provide a lot more than just recreational activity. It's estimated that the number of people who eat food grown in urban farms or community gardens is in the hundreds of millions across the globe.

There are some who think the idea is all just a passing fashion and that the new garden will soon become ugly and overgrown, and won't be maintained properly. They should take a look again a few years from now. It's amazing what we can achieve when we work together and support each other.

The community gardening movement is no passing fashion. During the Second World War everyone in Britain was urged to 'Dig for Victory' by growing vegetables in every bit of spare land. Backyards and nature strips were dug up in the struggle to keep families fed. In the crisis of war, people suddenly understood how vulnerable a society is if we have forgotten or never learned how to produce our own food.

Many of those same community gardens are still there. The Queen herself has converted some land at Buckingham Palace into a food garden, just as vegies were grown there in her childhood, during the war. And in America the First Lady has started growing food in the grounds of the White House.

Now we are facing a different sort of crisis. It is pretty obvious that vegetables that arrive on your family's table by the 'slow' method, grown from seed in your own local garden, are going to be better for your health, but what some people don't see is that when we grow our own fresh food it is much less likely to be tossed out. When you've grown it yourself, you value it. If there's too much to eat, you don't throw it out: you share it with others. So everybody benefits.

People are used to making many trips in their many cars to pick up processed and packaged food. They are used to hopping into their cars to get takeaway food for their families too. Not only are these car trips bad for the environment but convenience food carries a hidden price tag because a lot of it is wasted and ends up in landfill, adding to environmental damage.

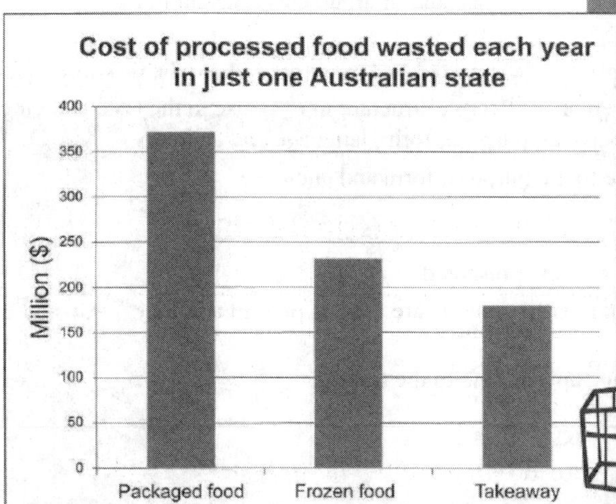

Data: NSW Environment Protection Authority

This is unsustainable. It's time we started to grow and use fresh food in a way that will benefit our planet, as well as ourselves.

And let's not forget the many other benefits to be gained from the activity of gardening. Primary schools across our state are establishing food gardens because it's a great way for children to learn. Most of us can remember our Dad or Grandpa showing us how to put seeds in the earth and water them in. We might remember the satisfaction of the first harvest. Our kids spend far too much time indoors and nothing could be healthier for them than doing some physical work in the fresh air, learning something that might even help them and their neighbourhood survive a food shortage one day. And they'll get to know their neighbours. Community gardening is for everyone not just those few individuals who enjoy a certain activity. There are no barriers. There is always plenty to share and nothing says 'friendship' like a gift of homegrown fresh food.

We urge the Council to take the visionary step of voting for the garden. To you, the community, we say join in! Tell the Council you support the idea and help us make this a success. Opportunities like this don't come along often. It is a rare chance for all of us to get together and work towards a common goal, to 'Dig for Victory' again – this time for a healthier future, for ourselves, our children and our planet.

Examination assessment criteria

The examination will address all the criteria. Student responses will be assessed against the following criteria.

Section C – Analysis of language use

- understanding of the ideas and points of view presented
- analysis of ways in which language and visual features are used to present a point of view and to persuade readers
- controlled and effective use of language appropriate to the task

EAL Section C – Analysis of language use

Instructions for Section C

Section C consists of **two** parts.

Parts 1 and 2 are equally weighted.

Carefully read the material below and then complete **both** parts 1 and 2.

Your response will be assessed according to the criteria set out in this book.

Section C is worth 30 marks.

TASK

Part 1

Write a note-form summary of the newsletter that is found on the following page.

Your response must be in **note form**. Do not use complete sentences.

Part 2

Write a piece of prose that explains how language and visual features have been used in the newsletter to attempt to persuade the readers about **three** of the main points of the newsletter.

Background information

A community has been discussing possible future uses for an area of land that has not been used since the closure of a railway line. The local city council owns the land and will decide how the land should be used. The Grow Slow Garden Group has proposed that the land be used for a community garden.

The leader of the Grow Slow Garden Group has produced a newsletter, as shown below. Before the council's decision is made, this newsletter will be distributed to every household in the local area.

Getting our future back on the rails – slowly

As everyone knows, the Council is about to decide what to do with the disused railway yards near our city centre. At present this land is just an ugly place where some inconsiderate people dump rubbish. Everyone has had the chance to suggest ideas, including those who want the land fenced and concreted over to use for skateboarding or for yet another car park. We hope the Council will decide in favour of a community garden.

However, there has been a lot of misinformation and misguided comment. This newsletter aims to correct any misunderstanding and give you accurate information.

Some people who object to the proposed garden seem to think the idea comes from a radical group of environmentalists. There's nothing extreme about the Grow Slow group and we are proud to be contributing to a greener Australia. In fact it's time the Council took notice of international trends and approved our plan to transform this shockingly neglected wasteland into fresh, natural land.

This is a forward-thinking Council and it has the chance to bring us up to date with the rest of the world. City farms and cooperative, shared gardens are common in other countries. And they can be surprisingly productive. It might seem like a hobby but these small gardens provide a lot more than just recreational activity. It's estimated that the number of people who eat food grown in urban farms or community gardens is in the hundreds of millions across the globe.

There are also some who think our idea is just a passing fashion. Community gardening is not just a passing fashion. During the Second World War, everyone in Britain was encouraged to 'Dig for Victory' by growing vegetables in every bit of spare land – backyards, nature strips and vacant land were all dug up in the struggle to keep families fed. In the crisis of war, people suddenly understood that their society was vulnerable if they couldn't produce their own food.

In more recent times in Britain the Queen herself has converted some land at Buckingham Palace into a food garden, just as it was during the war when she was young. And in America the First Lady has started growing food in the grounds of the White House.

Poster displayed in Britain in World War II

Now, 70 years after the Second World War, we are facing a different sort of crisis. It is obvious that the vegetables that arrive on your family's table by the 'slow' method, grown from seed in your own local garden, are going to be better for your health. What some people don't see is that when we grow our own fresh food, it is much less likely to be wasted or thrown out. When you've grown your own food, you value it. If there's too much to eat, you don't throw it out: you share it with others. So everybody benefits.

People are used to making many trips to the shops in their many cars to buy processed or packaged food. They are used to hopping into their cars to get takeaway food for their families too. Not only are these car trips bad for the environment but convenience food carries a hidden price tag because a lot of it becomes waste in a rubbish bin. This adds to environmental damage.

We can't go on like this. It's time we started to grow and use fresh food in a way that will benefit our planet, as well as ourselves.

And let's not forget the many other benefits from the activity of gardening. A lot of primary schools have food gardens because they are a great way to learn. Most of us can remember our Dad or Grandfather showing us how to put seeds in the earth and to water them in. We might remember the satisfaction of our first home-grown vegetables. Our kids spend far too much time indoors and nothing could be healthier for them than doing some physical work in the fresh air. Learning how to grow their own food might help them and others to survive if there is a food shortage in the future. And they'll get to know their neighbours. Community gardening is for everyone. There is always plenty to share and nothing says 'friendship' like a gift of home-grown fresh food.

So to you, the community, we say join in! Tell the Council you support the idea and help us make this a success. It is a rare chance for all of us to get together and work towards the same goal, to 'Dig for Victory' again – this time for a healthier future for ourselves, our children and our planet.

Examination assessment criteria

The examination will address all the criteria. Student responses will be assessed against the following criteria.

Section C – Analysis of language use

- understanding of the ideas and points of view in the material presented
- analysis of ways in which language and visual features are used to present a point of view and to persuade readers
- control of the mechanics of the English language to support meaning

Chapter 12

Suggested responses to the VCAA 2013 English exams

Section C – Analysis of language use

Mainstream response

The closure of a railway line in a local community has generated discussion as to the future uses of the land the line occupied. The leader of the Grow Slow Garden Group has produced a newsletter entitled 'Getting our future back on the rails – slowly', for all householders in the local area contending that the land be dedicated to a community garden that would witness the 'transformation' of the 'shockingly neglected wasteland into fresh, natural land'. In a sincere and optimistic tone, the leader of the group urges residents to request that the local Council, who owns the land, recognise the importance of converting the space into a garden for the sake of future generations who will benefit 'from the activity of gardening'. The accompanying visuals support his contention as they promote the tradition of sustainable agricultural practices and highlight the 'cost of processed food wasted each year' in Australia. The leader uses a logical and frank style in an attempt to motivate his target audience to 'help … make [the garden] a success'.

The inclusive nature of the title alerts the readers to their involvement in the progress of establishing a healthier and more eco-friendly time ahead for their community. The play on words – the suggestion that the community should get 'back on the rails' in relation to a positive social and environmental use of the railway land – implies that a solution has already been found by the Grow Slow Garden Group, assuring householders that they need only support the group to contribute to a 'greener Australia'. The writer disapprovingly provides a list of the undesirable elements of the current state of the land, which is 'currently only good for rats, snakes and those few anti-social citizens who think that it's acceptable to dump rubbish illegally'. This is coupled with an inventory of other suggestions for the use of the land such as it being 'fenced and concreted over and used for skateboarding or for yet another car park', in order to reinforce the 'misguided comment[s]' by 'some people' who 'objected to the proposed garden'. In doing this, the writer compels his audience to recognise that a more positive use of the land must be supported, and implies that any other plan for the land would be unwise.

The writer rationally asserts that the purpose of his newsletter is to 'clear the air and set the record straight', reassuringly stating that Grow Slow are 'proud' to be introducing this action and are not 'extreme' or 'radical … environmentalists', but are bringing to the notice of the Council the necessity to 'transform [the] shockingly neglected wasteland into fresh, natural land'. This may serve to encourage householders to act in such a way that they too will feel 'proud' to contribute to literally 'clearing the air' within their community.

The leader of Grow Slow approvingly congratulates the Council on being 'forward-thinking' in order to show that he believes that they, and the householders who should therefore support them, have the wherewithal to bring the community 'up to date with the rest of the world' by taking 'notice of international trends' and instating a community garden. He repeatedly separates himself and his audience from detractors by referring to 'some people' who objected to the garden and 'some who think that the idea is all just a passing fashion'. He uses evidence from the Second World War 'Dig for Victory' campaign to affirm the benefits of sustainably providing food for families within the community. The image of the 'Dig for Victory' poster, reminiscent of the war enlistment posters, attempts to recruit families to fight for what's important in life – rosy-cheeked children who should be fed vegetables 'for their [health's] sake'. This emotive appeal to parental responsibility and social conscience is supported by references to the 'hundreds of millions' of people 'across the globe', including 'the Queen herself', and 'in America the First Lady', who promote garden-grown produce. Community members are likely to be persuaded to advocate for a garden within their own council area as they respond to the notion that a society who doesn't 'learn' how to produce its own food is 'vulnerable' if they cannot sustain themselves during a 'crisis'.

Grow Slow's leader presents householders with a 'different sort of crisis' as he highlights that processed and packaged food 'carries a hidden price tag' as a significant portion of it is 'wasted and ends up in landfill, adding to environmental damage'. These appeals to the public's hip-pocket and environmental conscience are reinforced by a NSW Environment Protection Authority graph detailing the 'cost of processed food wasted each year in just one Australian state'. The use of these expert statistics generates support for the community garden program from an audience concerned for both the health of their wallets and the future of the Earth. The writer logically argues that it's 'pretty obvious' that locally grown vegetables 'are going to be better for [the] health' of community members. The use of the rhetorical question accompanying the graph, 'What price does Planet Earth have to pay for your convenience?', incites a sense of guilt within an audience who probably have not considered that value needs to be placed on 'sharing' food 'with others' to ensure that 'everybody benefits', prompting them to want to grow their own food so as not to harm the Earth.

The writer appeals to nostalgia when expressing that most of his audience will 'remember [their] Dad or Grandpa showing [them] how to put seeds in the earth and water them in'. As community members 'might remember the satisfaction of [their] first harvest', Grow Slow's leader presents a sentimental argument to his audience who will be encouraged to once again find satisfaction through supporting a community garden. He again appeals to parental concerns for the health of 'our kids' who will reap the benefits of 'the activity of gardening', as they are compellingly reminded that their 'kids spend far too much time indoors'.

The leader of the Grow Slow Garden Group concludes his newsletter by 'urging' the Council to take the 'visionary step of voting for the garden'. In a positive and enthusiastic tone he requests that the community 'join in', persuading them to tell the Council that they too want to be part of the 'visionary' action group that will make the garden a 'success'. His final inclusive statement is likely to convince householders that this is a 'rare' chance for them to 'get together and work towards a common goal', influencing them to take the 'opportunity' to be instrumental in creating a 'healthier future, for ourselves, our children and our planet'.

NB: When you are uncertain about the gender of the author, simply nominate a gender and use it consistently throughout your analysis, e.g. the leader/he/his/himself. Do not write he/she or switch genders in your analysis.

EAL Section C – Analysis of language use

Part 1 response

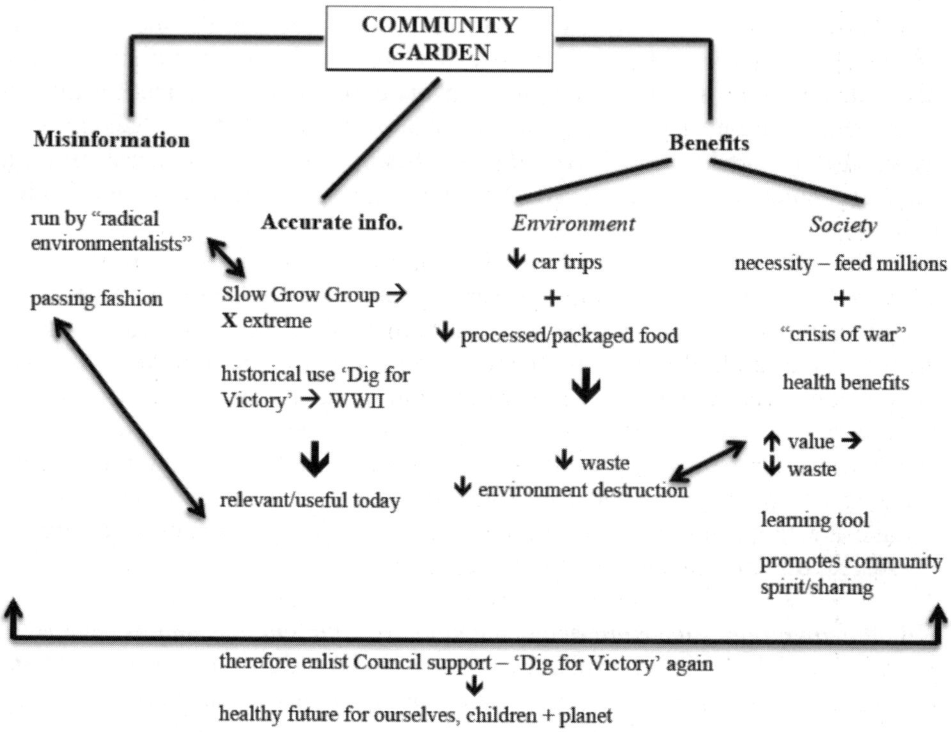

Part 2 response

The newsletter, 'Getting our future back on the rails – slowly', appeals to the local city council to transform a disused railway line into a community garden. In a reasonable tone, the Grow Slow Garden Group proposes that the introduction of a community garden would provide many benefits. As the newsletter will be distributed to every household in the local area, the target audience is most likely residents in the community, as well as Council members.

The Grow Slow Garden group begins by pointing out that those who object to the proposed garden are misguided. They confidently reassure the reader that there is 'nothing extreme' about their intentions in order to establish the reader's trust early on. Furthermore, claims that they are a 'radical group of environmentalists' are immediately rejected so the group establishes credibility. Readers are likely to believe that the group is reasonable as a result.

The Grow Slow Garden Group acknowledges the benefits of community gardens, pointing to their important role in history. Using an appeal to tradition, the Grow Slow Garden Group opposes the claims of critics that community gardening is merely 'a passing fashion', instead emphasising its ability to sustain during times of 'crisis'. Here, the group refers to the 'Dig for Victory' movement which encouraged Britons to utilise 'backyards, nature strips and vacant land' in order to survive during resource shortages in the Second World War. After reading that sustainable living is still as relevant today as it was 70 years ago, the readers are likely to feel reassured that they too can avoid food shortages and live well. This will mean a 'victory' for their future. The poster also reiterates the advantages of the 'Dig For Victory' movement. The background of the poster shows the smiling faces of children who have obviously benefitted from home-grown vegetables. In addition, the slogan, 'For their sake, grow your own vegetables", claims that home grown vegetables are necessary for a child to thrive. Readers who are parents will be keen to ensure their child's well-being and will therefore consider growing their food.

Finally, the Grow Slow Garden Group emphatically states that environmental damage can be avoided with more sustainable practices such as growing 'our own fresh food'. In order to strengthen this idea, a graph, provided by the NSW Environmental Protection Authority, clearly demonstrates the significant cost associated with the waste of processed food. The hard evidence may arouse dismay within residents who will be appalled by the 'hidden price tag' associated with the waste. In addition, some residents may feel a sense of guilt as their needless 'trips to the shops' are contributing to environmental damage. Moreover, the accompanying rhetorical question, 'What price does the earth have to pay for your convenience?' challenges the reader to think deeply about the implications of their actions. Not only will they reconsider their consumption of 'processed or packaged food' but they may adopt the view that growing fresh food instead will directly 'benefit our planet'.

Chapter 13

VCAA 2014 English exams

Section C – Analysis of language use

Instructions for Section C
Section C requires students to analyse the use of written and visual language.
Read the material below and then complete the task below.
Write your analysis as a coherently structured piece of prose.
Your response will be assessed according to the criteria set out in this book.
Section C is worth one-third of the total assessment for the examination.

TASK
How is written and visual language used in the newspaper article and the letter to attempt to persuade readers to share the points of view presented in them?

Background information
Yvette Yergon's opinion piece, 'Exploring our dreams', was published in the opinion pages of a daily newspaper. Dr Peter Laikis wrote a letter to the editor with the title, 'Off the planet'. This was later published. Both pieces are reproduced below.

Exploring our dreams

Yvette Yergon

Space is not as far away as you might think – only about 160 kilometres straight up. If you live in Victoria, you are closer to space than you are to Canberra. Space exploration has been on my mind this week after visiting an exhibition presented by an international group known as *Kolombus-21*. This is a group of influential thinkers who have been urging governments across the globe to pool resources and collaborate on further space exploration in the twenty-first century.

Touring the exhibition reminded me how inspiring exploration can be. It seems to be in our nature to dream about what's beyond the world we know, and setting out to explore the unknown is the biggest thing we do. The great explorer Christopher Columbus set off in a wooden ship powered by nothing but wind and with only his own skill and courage and the stars to guide him. That's pretty inspiring.

Most of us rightly admire the bravery of astronauts who, six centuries later, have taken the risk of exploring beyond Earth and have given us such a different perspective on the beautiful blue planet we call home.

But to get governments interested in spending the huge amount of money needed for space exploration, there must be more to it than the thrill of discovery. Perhaps there's a new mining boom waiting to happen in space, with people looking for more of the minerals we know well and maybe some we haven't dreamed of yet.

Evidently there are virtually unlimited resources out there for the taking because nobody owns them. A company recently set out to claim ownership of an asteroid, surprising the United Nations because there are no laws about ownership in space.

It's easy to understand why someone might want to own one of those lifeless rocks. An asteroid with the unromantic name '1986DA' suddenly became very interesting when scientists reported that it contains about 10,000 tons of gold and 10 times that much platinum, to the value of about a trillion dollars.
Unfortunately this one is quite a long way off – about 32 million kilometres – but that doesn't seem to dampen anyone's enthusiasm.

'Well, OK, it might be only a dream right now,' said one young exhibition guide, gazing up at some spectacular star images, 'but one day it will come true. We've got to find answers to our problems to protect the future of life on Earth. That means taking risks and encountering the unexpected, but good things always come out of that.' Columbus certainly encountered the unexpected – he expected to sail through to India and bumped into North and South America instead. And I agree that good things can come from exploring the unknown. A lot of the valuable products available to us now are the direct result of research associated with space programs of the last few decades, benefits that nobody predicted at the time.

Kolombus-21 talks a lot about international cooperation. This hasn't always been a feature of space exploration, but now that we have an international space station supported by 15 nations, the era of collaboration seems to be well established. If there was ever a good time to turn more of the unknown into useful knowledge, it might be now. There's a strong view that it's time to inspire the next generation of scientists. Every government knows we've got to do that, just as we've got to invest in the next generation of technology. That's where the answers to our problems are really going to come from.

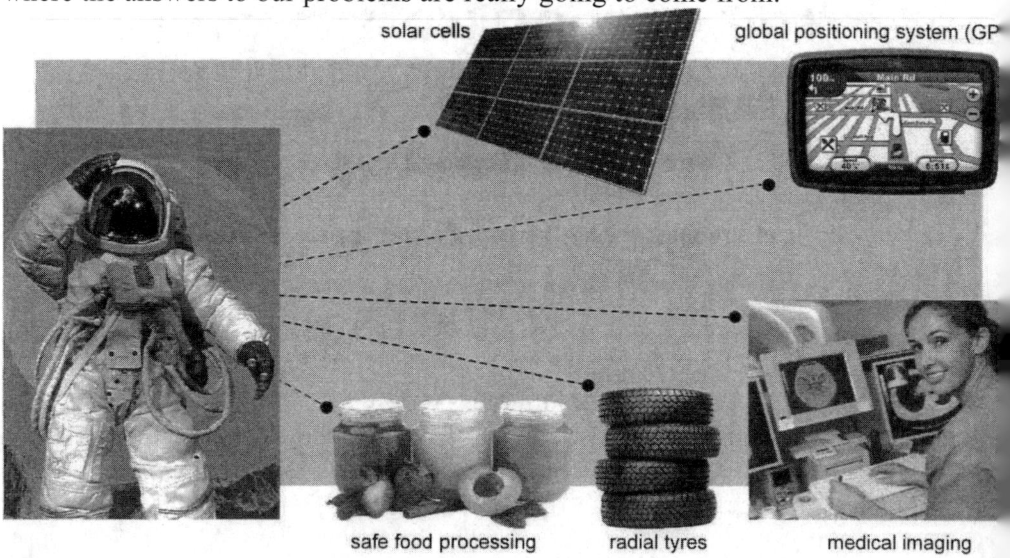

'And the name of the group,' I asked the guide at the end of the tour, 'it's in honour of Columbus?' 'Partly,' he smiled, 'It also means "dove".'
The international symbol of peace. I could see the point. It's important to recharge our scientific batteries and get the next big thing going in space exploration – possibly a voyage to Mars. But it must be done for the whole planet and for peaceful purposes. Perhaps with big dreamers like *Kolombus-21* behind it, it might even turn out that way.

Off the planet

Thanks, Yvette Yergon, for drawing our attention to the ‘next big thing’. For a while there we were wasting our time thinking about little issues like hunger and disease and the environment. But no, let's spend a few trillions more on the illusion that we can solve our problems by leaving Earth and finding somewhere better.

Wake up, Yvette! When did governments or kings or emperors ever fund exploration for peaceful purposes or the good of the world? The voyages of Columbus were powered more by greed than by wind. The ‘dreams’ involved were of more and more wealth.

Seems like nothing much has changed. Reality is, we don’t have to go into space looking for lifeless rocks. We just have to make sure that our infinitely precious blue planet doesn’t turn into one.

You know what I find truly inspiring? The idea of getting all the governments in the world to agree to keep working together on our real problems, one by one, step by step, until they are solved.

OK, that might be only a dream right now – but at least it's a dream worth pursuing.

Dr Peter Laikis

Examination assessment criteria

Section C – Analysis of language use

- understanding of the ideas and points of view presented
- analysis of ways in which language and visual features are used to present a point of view and to persuade readers
- controlled and effective use of language appropriate to the task

EAL Section C – Analysis of language use

Instructions for Section C
Section C consists of **two** parts. Parts 1 and 2 are equally weighted. Carefully read the material below and then complete **both** parts 1 and 2. Your response will be assessed on according to the criteria set out in this book. Section C is worth 30 marks.

TASK

Part 1
Write a note-form summary of the article '**Exploring our dreams**' found below.
Your response must in **note form**. Do not use complete sentences.

Part 2
Write a piece of prose that explains how language and visual features have been used to attempt to persuade the readers about **three** of the main points in any part of the material below. You may choose point in '**Exploring our dreams**' or '**Off the planet**' or both.

Background information
Yvette Yergon writes for a newspaper. Recently she viewed an exhibition on space exploration presented by an international group of thinkers known as *Kolombus-21*. Her article 'Exploring our dreams' presents her response to the exhibition. The letter to the editor titled 'Off the planet' was sent to the newspaper after the article was published. It gives the views of one reader.

Use only the article 'Exploring our dreams' for your note form summary.

Exploring our dreams

Yvette Yergon

Space is not as far away as it seems. If you live in Victoria, you are closer to space than you are to Canberra. Space is only about 160 kilometres straight up. I've been thinking about space exploration this week after I had the pleasure of visiting an exhibition presented by an international group known as *Kolombus-21*. This is a group of influential thinkers who have been encouraging governments across the world to work together on space exploration in the twenty-first century.

After looking at the displays in the exhibition I was reminded of how inspiring exploration can be. It seems to be in human nature to dream about what's beyond the world we know. Setting out to explore the unknown is the biggest thing we do. After all, the great fifteenth-century explorer Christopher Columbus set off in a wooden ship, powered only by the wind, with only his own skill and courage and the stars to guide him. That's pretty inspiring.

Six centuries later, most of us rightly admire the bravery of astronauts who have taken the risk of exploring beyond Earth.

But space exploration costs a lot of money. Governments need reasons other than the thrill of discovery if they are going to spend the huge amounts of money needed to continue exploring in space. Perhaps there's a new mining boom waiting to happen in space, with people looking for more of the minerals we already know and maybe some we haven't dreamed of yet.

Evidently there are almost unlimited mineral resources out there in space, waiting to be claimed, and nobody owns them. The United Nations was surprised recently when a company tried to claim ownership of an asteroid. There aren't any laws about property ownership in space. It is easy to understand why people might be interested in these lifeless rocks. Recently scientists reported on an asteroid that contains about 10,000 tons of gold and even more platinum, to the value of about a trillion dollars. Unfortunately it is about 32 million kilometres away, but that doesn't seem to stop people dreaming.

One day such dreams might come true. This exhibition helped me to realise that it is important to search for new answers to our problems to protect the future of life on Earth. That means taking risks and meeting the unexpected.

Columbus certainly met the unexpected. He expected to sail through to India but bumped into North and South America instead.

And of course good things can come out of exploring the unknown. Many countries have spent a lot on space exploration and plenty of products we use today were developed from research associated with space programs. These benefits could not have been predicted at the time of this investment in space exploration.

Kolombus-21 values international cooperation. Space exploration used to be more competitive than cooperative. That wasn't very helpful. Now we have an international space station supported by15 nations, so now is the time to explore further and turn the unknown into useful knowledge. There's a strong view that it's time to inspire the next generation of scientists. Every government knows we've got to do this, just as we've got to invest in the next generation of technology. That's where the answers to the world's big problems are going to come from.

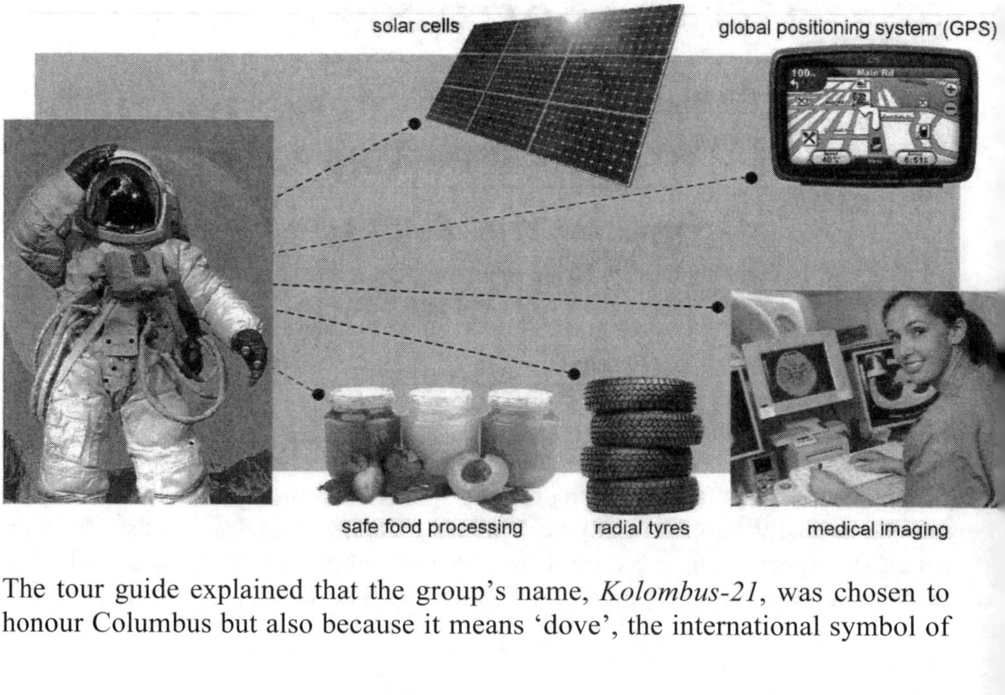

The tour guide explained that the group's name, *Kolombus-21*, was chosen to honour Columbus but also because it means 'dove', the international symbol of peace. I can see the point. Future space exploration must be done for the whole planet and for peaceful purposes. Perhaps with big dreamers like *Kolombus-21* working towards this goal we can be confident that it will happen in this way.

This letter to the editor was sent to the newspaper after the article was published.

Off the planet

Yvette Yergon seems to think we can solve the big problems of the world, such as hunger, disease and the environment, by leaving Earth and finding somewhere better. She wants governments to spend trillions of dollars based on this false belief.

Wake up, Yvette! When did governments or kings or emperors ever spend money on exploring for peaceful purposes or the good of the world? Columbus's ships were driven by greed as well as wind. People's dreams were of more and more wealth. Nothing seems to have changed. Today's challenge is to make sure that the precious planet we call home doesn't become like a lifeless asteroid.

You know what I find truly inspiring? The idea of getting all the governments in the world to agree to keep working together on our problems on Earth, one by one, until they are solved. This might be only a dream now – but it's a dream worth pursuing.

Peter Laikis

Examination assessment criteria

Section C – Analysis of language use

- understanding of the ideas and points of view presented
- analysis of ways in which language and visual features are used to present a point of view and to persuade readers
- control of the mechanics of the English language to support meaning

Chapter 14

Suggested responses to the VCAA 2014 English exams

Section C – Analysis of language use

Sample 1 Language analysis response – semi weave structure

Prompted by visiting an exhibition presented by 'a group of influential thinkers', *Kolumbus-21*, Yvette Yergon writes an opinion piece for an audience of newspaper readers interested in opportunities for the growth of society. She aligns herself with the sentiments of *Kolumbus-21* and contends, in an optimistic tone, that governments should 'collaborate on space exploration in the twenty-first century'. The straightforward and affirmative style of Yergon's piece is complemented by the inclusion of two graphic images. Dr Peter Laikis has responded in opposition to Yergon's opinion piece through a letter to the editor published in the same daily newspaper. In an incredulous and scornful tone, he asserts that Yergon's perspective is 'Off the planet' and that governments must work together to address the world's 'real problems'.

Yergon introduces her viewpoint through the inclusive title 'Exploring our dreams', positively supporting her belief that it is 'in our nature to dream about what's beyond the world we know'. Through the repetition of the words 'inspiring', and 'dreams', readers are encouraged to see exploration as something accessible that should be actively pursued. Yergon favourably associates Christopher Columbus' 'skill and courage' with the 'bravery of astronauts' who have 'taken the risk of exploring beyond Earth' in order to position readers to see their actions as indispensable in providing a 'different perspective' on the 'planet [they] call home'.

By approvingly stating that most of her readers 'rightly admire' these astronauts, Yergon persuades those readers who may not see the necessity for continued exploration of other planets to acknowledge that the same admiration must be felt for space exploration. The accompanying image of the ship setting forth into the sunset, presumably to explore unchartered territory, echoes Columbus' voyage of discovery and presents readers with the romantic notion of a journey that may encounter the 'unexpected', revealing the 'good things' – such as the discovery of North and South America – that 'can come from exploring the unknown'. With a 'nothing ventured, nothing gained' attitude,

Yergon continues to position her readers to recognise that 'taking risks', as Columbus and astronauts have done in the past, can result in positive outcomes for all.

Yergon presents a united dream through the inclusive 'we', and the benefits of space exploration for all, as she rationally reminds her audience that many 'valuable products available to us now are the direct result of [unpredicted] research associated with space programs'. Through the focal point of the second graphic, an astronaut, with lines emanating from his body connecting to images of 'solar panels', a 'GPS system', 'radial tyres', 'medical imaging' and 'safe food processing', the readers' attention is drawn to the 'good things' that Yergon offers up as evidence as to the necessity for supporting future space exploration. The readers are coaxed to consider a world without such essential items and consequently acknowledge the significance of space exploration.

Yergon advocates a collaborative approach to research that should 'inspire the next generation of scientists.' In a bid to appeal to future knowledge and the development of 'the next generation of technology', Yergon leaves no doubt for the readers that 'the answers to our problems' are going to come from the 'next generation'. Readers are therefore encouraged to support the security of the nation's scientific progress through their endorsement of government funded space-related programs.

Concluding her piece with a sentimental reflection on the genesis of the name *Kolumbis-21*, Yergon presents to readers that it is not only in honour of Columbus, but also translates to 'dove' – the international symbol of peace. Metaphorically, Yergon states that it is 'now time to recharge our scientific batteries' and provokes readers to consider space exploration as a voyage undertaken by society 'for the whole planet and for peaceful purposes'.

Challenging Yergon's views, Dr Peter Laikis is scathing in his response to her suggestion that money should be invested in space exploration. He mockingly suggests that spending 'a few trillions more on the illusion that we can solve our problems by leaving Earth and finding somewhere better', at the expense of 'little issues like hunger and disease and the environment' is 'Off the planet'.

By ironically listing the 'real' issues impacting on 'our infinitely precious blue planet' he persuades readers to recognise that Earth could actually be the 'lifeless rock' in the future. His direct call for Yergon to 'Wake up!' is a call to all readers who may have overlooked that space exploration is driven by materialism and that Columbus' journey was one 'powered more by greed than wind' and not the romantic and courageous journey that Yergon suggests. Like Yergon, Dr Laikis uses the repetition of the word 'dream', however, he uses it to highlight what he sees as self-indulgent fantasies versus the 'truly inspiring' dream of governments working together 'on our real problems, one by one, step by step, until they are solved'.

Yergon's progressive and upbeat opinion piece reveals to her audience the benefits of funding and supporting space exploration through an inclusive and enthusing examination of the opportunities generated for society via this 'courageous' and 'inspiring' practice. In contrast, Dr Laikis presents the necessity of focusing their attention on dreams 'worth pursuing' and acknowledging that committing more government funding to space programs only decreases support for 'real problems' on Earth.

Word count 871

Sample 2 Language analysis response – total weave structure

Space exploration is an issue that regularly surfaces in the media for many reasons. After visiting an exhibition by *Kolombus-21*, Yvette Yergon wrote an opinion piece, published in a daily newspaper, in which she contends that space exploration is 'inspiring' and promotes 'international cooperation' between governments and 'the next generation of scientists'. She combines an idealistic tone with positive language and links to 'courageous' explorers in a bid to encourage her readers to be forward thinking and 'big dreamers'. In stark contrast, in his letter to the editor entitled 'Off the planet', Dr Peter Laikis employs a sarcastic tone that condemns Yergon's 'dreams' as 'illusion' while he asserts that governments should unite and be more concerned about 'our real problems' on Earth.

Yergon begins her piece by motivating her readers about how 'inspiring' space exploration can be. She utilises positive language and the example of 'great explorer Christopher Columbus' to demonstrate to readers how 'taking risks' and 'encountering the unexpected' can benefit us. Yergon further emphasises this point by saying that Columbus explored in 'a wooden ship powered by nothing but wind' and cites his 'courage', 'skill' and 'the stars' as his guide. The accompanying image of a three-masted sailing ship on rough waters silhouetted against a large moon reinforces the inspiration of exploration.

Yergon links Columbus' exploration to the 'bravery' of astronauts prompting readers to think of them as modern-day Columbus figures whom we 'rightly admire' and who promote peace in the world. Dr Laikis, in turn, scoffs at her notion of 'exploration for peaceful purposes' and states that Columbus' voyages were 'powered more by greed' and the 'dreams' were of 'wealth'. This direct response serves to denigrate Yergon's assertions as incorrect and may result in his readers questioning whether space exploration is more idealistic than realistic. He appeals to his readers' sense of environmental preservation when he discredits Yergon's claim that some 'lifeless rocks' in space are actually worth millions and refers to the need to make sure that 'our precious blue planet' doesn't turn into a lifeless rock.

She claims that the positive outcomes of investment in space are more than just the 'thrill of discovery'. Yergon coaxes her readers to 'dream' as she presents the 'valuable products' associated with the space program in the form of an accompanying infographic. These products of 'solar cells', 'global positioning system', 'safe food processing', 'radial tyres' and 'medical imaging' are all linked by dotted lines to a saluting astronaut and serve to remind her readers of the benefits they enjoy due to space exploration. The graphic also supports her generalisation that 'every government knows' 'we've got to invest in the next generation of technology' and positions readers to think that space exploration is necessary in order to progress technologically and that it is where the 'answers to our problems' will be found. In a scathing attack, Dr Laikis refutes Yergon's proposal to fund space exploration when he sarcastically asserts that we have been wasting our time thinking about 'little issues like hunger and disease' when we should have been spending 'a few trillions' believing that we can solve our problems by space exploration. His pragmatic approach coupled with his blunt exclamation of 'Wake up, Yvette!' positions readers to doubt the realistic value of space exploration and may cause them to question the reality of Yergon's 'dreams'.

Yergon concludes her piece by positioning her readers to think that space exploration is an issue that is 'the next big thing', a 'whole planet' idea and conducive to 'peace'. She again refers to Columbus and emotively links the name of the 'influential thinkers' *Kolumbus-21* to a 'dove', the international symbol of 'peace'. However, Dr Laikis ridicules this by questioning the notion of what is 'truly inspiring' then offering his prudent and pragmatic idea that 'getting all governments' to agree to collaborate on 'our real problems' is the true dream and 'one worth pursuing'.

Yergon's opinion piece encourages readers to be 'inspired', 'dream' and share her optimistic stance and progressive view about the benefits of space exploration for humanity despite the cost. In contrast, Dr Laikis attempts to present a more realistic point of view while still striving for the betterment of humanity when he states that the current issues on Earth are far more important for peace and progression.

Word count 716

EAL Section C – Analysis of language use

Part 1 response

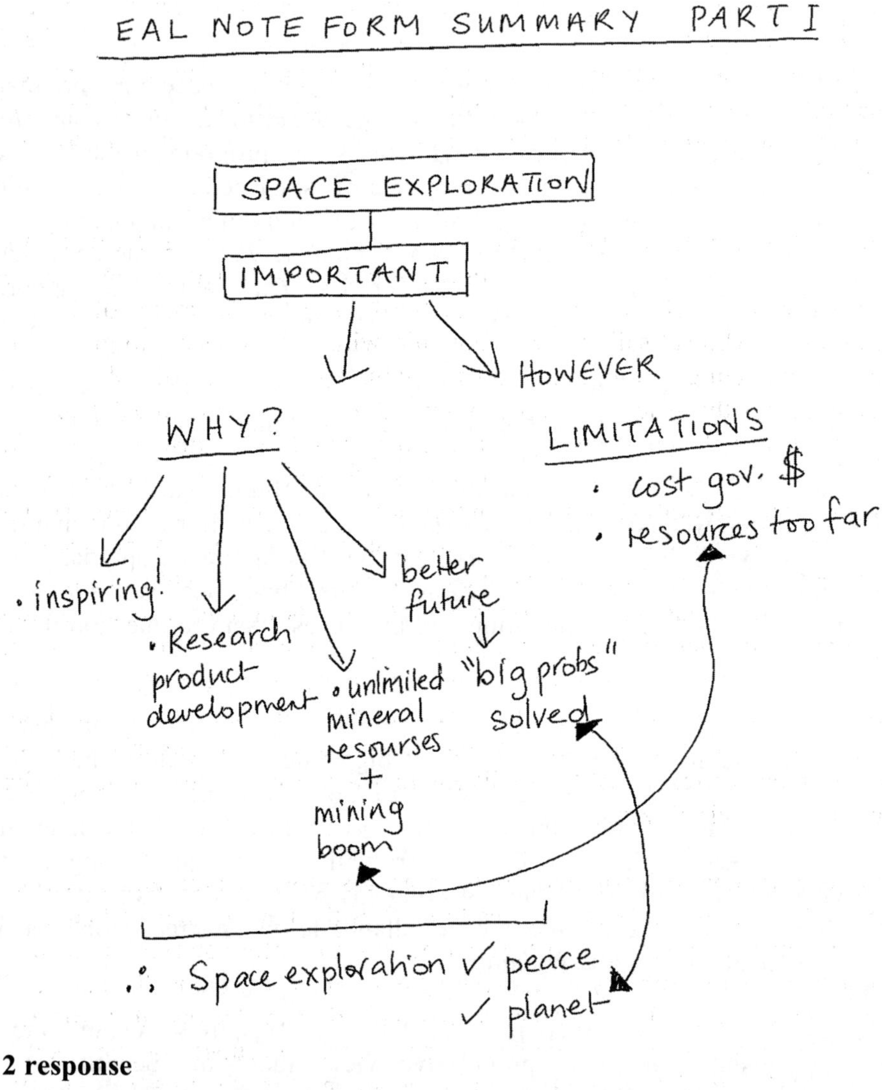

Part 2 response

In her article entitled 'Exploring our dreams', Yvette Yergon writes in response to an exhibition on space exploration presented by an international group of thinkers known as *Kolumbus-21*. In an enthusiastic tone, she contends that space exploration is vital in the twenty-first century as it will benefit the whole planet. In contrast, Peter Laikis' letter to the editor strongly argues that space exploration is unnecessary. As the articles have been published in a newspaper, the readership is going to be the general public, as well as members of the government.

Yergon begins by introducing *Kolumbus-21*, a group that has been encouraging governments to work together on space exploration in the twenty-first century. By highlighting that the group is made up of 'influential thinkers', she draws attention to the expertise and credentials of the group. This will automatically position readers (who are unfamiliar with the group) to accept that the information is reliable and the views being presented are worthy of their consideration.

Furthermore, Yergon outlines the importance of 'exploring the unknown'. In order to illustrate this point, she draws a comparison between the 'bravery of the astronauts', who explore beyond Earth, and the 'courage' of Christopher Columbus, who set sail in a wooden ship with only the stars to guide him. An image depicting Columbus' boat against the force of Mother Nature accompanies the article. It serves to remind readers of Columbus' determination and his survival against the odds. These inspiring tales of discovery are likely to fill the readers with a sense of wonder, at the same time encouraging them to accept that exploration is a worthwhile activity. Moreover, Yergon claims that research associated with space programs has yielded 'plenty of products that we use today'. She provides photographs of these valuable inventions (such as solar cells, medical imaging, radial tyres and GPS), linking their origins to the space program. Members of the general public might be impressed by this information as they consider the direct benefits to their lives. Finally, Yergon appeals to all governments 'to invest in the next generation of technology', in the hope that they will find the answers to the 'world's big problems'. In response, government officials will most likely feel a sense of duty to act in the best interests of their citizens.

Laikis responds to Yergon's article in an assertive fashion and systematically rebuts her arguments. His bold headline, 'Off the planet', signals that Yergon is out of touch with reality and that her beliefs are unfounded. In order to further undermine her credibility he addresses her directly, emphatically stating, 'Wake up, Yvette!'. Here he urges her to pay attention to the fact that governments have never spent money 'exploring for peaceful purposes or the good of the world'. After reading this attack on his opponent, the reader is likely to question Yergon's knowledge of the issue and feel inclined to side with Laikis. In addition, Laikis warns that today's challenge is to ensure that our planet does not become like 'a lifeless asteroid'. He employs a simile to fill the reader with a sense of dread, leaving them to ponder the threat to their 'precious planet'.

The author and publisher wish to thank the following sources for permission to reproduce material:

Images: Shutterstock.com / BVA, **pp.193, 197** / eddtoro, **pp.194, 198(astronaut)** / Best3d, **pp.194, 198 (solar cells)** / 3d brained, **pp.194, 198 (GPS)** / Monkey Business Images, **pp.194, 198 (medical imaging)** / Dmitry Kalinovsky, **pp.194, 198 (tyres)** / margouillat photo, **pp.194, 198 (food)**.

1. Persuasive language and techniques

Logical

Expert opinion: use of titles and expertise can impress a reader (e.g. 'Associate Prof Bines, of The Royal Children's Hospital, stated that … ').

Statistics: figures, percentages can strengthen an argument (e.g. '30% of VCE students admit they smoke').

Facts: objective, proven statements carry great weight in an argument.

Rhetorical questions: a dramatic question that doesn't need an answer because the answer is already understood (e.g. 'Do patients need to die before the government acts?'). Used to highlight a point (e.g. the lack of action by the government on this issue), and position the reader to agree with the writer.

Repetition: repeated words and images can be used to emphasise a point and reinforce an argument.

2. Persuasive language and techniques

Visual

Composition: number of items/subjects and their position within the text and in relation to one another. It includes camera angles, body language, white space.

Body text: words within frame of text (e.g. speech bubbles, signs).

Caption: words outside frame of text (can state contention).

Motifs/symbols/icons: signature signs or labels that identify a subject. Images that represent ideas or concepts (e.g. rose represents love, dove represents peace). An icon is a symbol or image of a sacred or religious subject. Sydney Opera House, Phar Lap are Australian icons. Appeals to audience values.

Style: the way the creator constructs the text (e.g. minimal number of strokes and big round heads for a cartoon).

Layout: different font sizes and percentage of text that is graphics. Can make message clearer to audience.

3. Persuasive language and techniques

Emotive

Appeals: to family or social values, groups, tradition, emotion, national identity, logic, etc. Designed to gain an emotional response. Plays on people's values, beliefs, loyalties and emotions.

Generalisations: appeals to reader's general sense or may select prevailing prejudices and seek to exclude those who do not agree. Start with 'all' or 'every'.

Anecdote: a story from personal experience. Personalises a text and can have emotional appeal.

Inclusive language: seeks to include certain people by making reader feel like an outsider if they don't agree (e.g. 'we', 'all Australians', 'ours', 'us').

Personal attacks: comments that seek to undermine arguments offered by opposing persons (e.g. 'anti-social hippies and bludgers').

4. General analysis tips

1. Identify the issue.
2. Describe the catalyst – incident or event that sparked the issue.
3. State writer's contention.
4. Say *how* writers use persuasive techniques, language (including visual) and structure to position the audience and to convey their point of view.
5. What is the likely impact on their audience?
6. Avoid labelling (listing) persuasive techniques and language.
7. Follow the **Six steps to language analysis**.
8. Write language analysis using *formal* language and structure.
9. You cannot analyse everything.
10. Do not include your opinion on the issue.

5. Key words for language analysis

1. exaggeration
2. argument
3. opinion
4. definitely
5. writer
6. interpret
7. controversial
8. aggressive
9. sentence
10. environment

6. Exam hints

1. Exam stress is normal – find ways to deal with stress, e.g. exercise, meditation, deep breathing.
2. Examiners set exams for you to show what you can do.
3. Good exam preparation is rewarded.
4. Devise a plan of attack for the exam and stick to it!
5. Do practice exams and write essays under timed conditions.
6. Take a dictionary (decent and recent).
7. Take highlighters and/or different coloured pens.
8. Read all instructions carefully, including the background information in Section C.
9. Keep in mind assessment criteria.
10. Editing is important. There's no such thing as leftover time in an English exam!